TRAVEL

Fit & Healthy

Fodor's fyi

Fodor's Travel Publications
New York • Toronto • London • Sydney • Auckland
www.fodors.com

Editors: Karen Cure, Mark Sullivan

Managing Editors: Karen Watts, Lisa DiMona, Robin Dellabough

Editorial Contributor: Rachel Hoyt

Production/manufacturing: Publications Development Company of Texas

Cover Photo: PhotoDisc

Cover Design: Guido Caroti

Interior Design: Lisa Sloane

A Lark Production

ISBN 0-676-90115-8

ISSN 1533-1539

Important Tip

Although all prices, opening times, and other details in this book are based on
information supplied to us at press time, changes occur all the time in the travel
world, and Fodor's cannot accept responsibility for facts that become outdated or
for inadvertent errors or omissions. So always confirm information when it
matters, especially if you're making a detour to visit a specific place.

Special Sales

Fodor's Travel Publications are available at special discounts for bulk purchases
for sales promotions or premiums. Special editions, including personlized covers,
excerpts of existing guides, and corporate imprints, can be created in large
quantities for special needs. For more information, contact your local bookseller
or write to Special Markets, Fodor's Travel Publications, 280 Park Avenue, New
York, NY 10017. Inquiries from Canada should be directed to your local
Canadian bookseller or sent to Random House of Canada, Ltd., Marketing
Department, 2775 Matheson Boulevard East, Mississauga, Ontario L4W 4P7.
Inquiries from the United Kingdom should be sent to Fodor's Travel
Publications, 20 Vauxhall Bridge Road, London SW1V 2SA, England.

Printed in the United States of America

10 9 8 7 6 5 4 3 2 1

Contents

A Fit Approach to Travel

IMAGINE GETTING SO CAUGHT UP in your travels that you return feeling relaxed, rested, and inspired. It's a romantic notion, one shared by many travelers. But the reality is that any trip, whether it's a month-long safari in Africa or a two-day conference in Akron, can make you feel like you've been mowed down by the California Zephyr, and there's nothing romantic about that.

The way people approach travel has changed. In this work hard—play hard world, travelers are packing more and more into their vacations. In the corporate world, the very nature of business travel means juggling schedules, squeezing in meetings, running to catch planes. No wonder people return from trips sick, tired, and with a few extra pounds around their middles.

Here's the good news: with a little forethought, you can keep that mowed down feeling to a minimum. You can even return from your trip feeling better than when you left. This book will help you plan a trip with your health and fitness in mind. It includes strategies for preparing your body for the rigors of travel, taking care of yourself en route, exercising when you're on the go, and, perhaps most importantly, eating well when you're on the road. You'll find tips on how to stay in optimum physical, mental, and emotional condition on the road. You'll look and feel better while you're gone—and when you return. You'll have that extra pep to face whatever challenge comes your way. You'll feel more confident about that crucial business meeting, or have the stamina to enjoy a week with the kids at Walt Disney World. And it will be easier to get back into your regular healthy routine when you return home because you won't have left it behind in the first place.

RULES OF THE ROAD

Keep these guidelines in mind as you think about traveling fit and healthy:

Plan ahead

The key to having a healthy trip is basic: Do as much as you can in advance. Don't want to be stuck munching a bag of peanuts on your flight? Bring along your own healthy snacks. Wondering whether to bring your tennis racket? Ask the hotel where you'll find the closest court. A little forethought will give you all the tools you need to avoid that nasty Bermuda Triangle—fatigue, stress, and weight gain—that every traveler faces.

Be resourceful

Exercise is not always as easy to come by as popping into your hotel's health club for 45 minutes of aerobics—you might, for instance, find the health club closed for renovations. So be creative. You could take a brisk walk instead of your usual treadmill workout, or rent a bike instead of hopping on a stationary one. As long as you look around for smart ways to adapt, you'll never be far from your fitness goals.

Keep moving

If you do the math on how much time you spend sitting around when traveling—on airplanes, in restaurants, during business meetings—you'll realize you're more sedentary than when you're back home. Seek out opportunities to be active wherever you go, whether it's taking an hour-long walk around the airport during a layover or doing five minutes of jumping jacks in your hotel. Every move you make really adds up.

Ask for what you want

Always ask for exactly what you want, whether it's a room in a quieter part of the hotel or an entrée that's not on the menu. Don't be afraid you're being a pain in the neck. If you don't articulate what you want, chances are you won't get it. So don't just take what you can get—get what you really want.

Don't sabotage yourself

When traveling, it's a challenge to stay firmly in control of your own health and well-being. But when you identify your fitness goals and stick to them, the outcome of your trip isn't left up to chance. The trick to not sabotaging your healthy lifestyle boils down to asking yourself this: Is this something I'd do (or not do) at home?

Have fun

Staying healthy *should* be fun. Otherwise, why bother? So if you're killing yourself in order to stay on the straight and narrow, you're not doing it right. Don't just fixate on getting in your mandatory half hour on the cross-trainer; find fun ways to exercise in a new environment. Don't wince at every encounter with a restaurant menu; go ahead and live a little. Try something new, share a dessert, have a latte with whole milk every once in a while. Being healthy on the road doesn't have to be a drag. Keep your mind open to the possibilities—it's all in how you look at it.

2

Planning for a Healthy Trip

WHETHER YOU'RE OFF FOR A FROLIC in the sunny tropics or an extended stretch of business travel, it's just as important to plan for your health and fitness needs as it is to reserve a room or arrange for a rental car. The key to planning for healthy travel is to address diet, exercise, and medical requirements *before* you leave home. But what are your requirements? Have you ever really sat down and defined your health and fitness needs and goals? Identifying them beforehand allows you to seek out the information you need to plan.

YOUR HEALTH AND FITNESS REQUIREMENTS

Remember when you were young and your mother filled out those health forms at the beginning of every school year? She would list illnesses you had, allergies you suffered from, medication you were taking, and activities you were to avoid. Think of your adult health and fitness requirements as the grown-up version of that form. It's a statement of your health status and an advisory of your special needs, as well as an accounting of your regular fitness habits and activities.

Your physical state

Start by listing any conditions that affect your daily behavior in any way, anything from serious conditions like asthma and high blood pressure to more minor complaints like tendinitis in your elbow or calluses on your feet. You might not even think much about these conditions in your daily life, but it's critical to remember them as you make plans to travel. You need to be able to deal with them as effectively on the road as you do at home.

Your medical needs

Next note any of the ways you deal with your special needs—medications, ice packs, braces, or physical therapy.

TRAVEL LOG

When I decided to bring my husband and son to a two-day convention in Philadelphia, I assumed there wouldn't be a minute for my daily run. Wrong! The minute I saw Fairmount Park, which connects the Rodin Museum to the Philadelphia Art Museum in a lush, green, uninterrupted, car-free 5-mile loop, I *hated* myself for not bringing my running shoes. I learned my lesson once and for all: better to have my running stuff and not use it than want it and not have it.

—*Suzanne M., Stamford, Connecticut*

Your fitness regimen

Briefly write down what you usually do to stay fit—everything from running 5 miles a day or taking an aerobics class three times a week.

The elements we've outlined above add up to your Health and Fitness Requirements. Now that you have that picture, use it to begin planning for healthy travel.

The Fit List

Many travelers keep their important fitness and dietary goals in the back of their mind when traveling, but it's more effective to put them in writing. Determine what your daily fitness goals are, for example, walking at least 2 miles every day, or just keeping your hand out of the cookie jar. Make a list of the top five, write them down, and bring them with you every time

3 1833 03922 8421

SAMPLE FIT LIST

☐ Walk whenever possible.

☐ Eat smaller portions.

☐ Drink at least eight glasses of water.

☐ Stretch for 5 minutes every morning and evening.

☐ Do at least 20 minutes of aerobic exercise.

you travel. Whether you're going on a business trip to Fresno or a driving tour of France, pack your customized Fit List to help you stay on track.

If you can't do all of the items on your Fit List every day, don't feel guilty. The whole point of the list is to help keep you healthy and relieve stress, not add to it. The Fit List is a reminder to help you ward off those extra five pounds you might otherwise gain at an all-inclusive resort.

Your Eating Habits

Maintaining your weight while away from home can be tough because you have less control over what you eat and when you eat it. The trick is to stick as closely as possible to your normal routine. Think about your eating habits at home and how you can adapt them while you're traveling.

Many people give themselves permission to eat whatever they want while traveling, but this is a sure way to pack on the pounds. If your usual morning meal is a bagel and juice, don't head to the all-you-can-eat breakfast buffet while on the road. If you keep some healthful munchies in your desk at work, be sure to bring some along on that business trip. And it's just as bad to eat too little as to eat too much—your body is expecting its regular fuel schedule and won't take kindly to any drastic deviations. Skipping meals will leave you tired, hungry, and powerless against the snack machine or candy counter.

What should you do? As part of your Fit List, write down what and how you want to eat while on a trip. Remind yourself about the foods that are part of your normal diet. Most important of all, be mentally prepared to stick with whatever eating program you set out for yourself.

MEAT-FREE ZONE

Ask about a vegetarian entrée and too many restaurants will offer you a tossed salad. To avoid such meager meals, it's best to locate a real vegetarian restaurant before you travel. A Web site called vegdining.com touts itself as the "online guide to vegetarian dining around the world." It has a list of more than 1,000 meat-free eateries around the world.

Your Fitness Regimen

Just as you identified your eating habits, take a look at the way you exercise. Do you use weights or take dance classes? Do you exercise every day, every other day, or once a week? Plan to be consistent while you're on the road. If you are accustomed to aerobics twice a week, look for classes at your destination. No health club at your hotel? There are plenty of other options, such as heading to a nearby gym or finding the fitness channel on the television in your hotel room.

Again, the key is to stick as closely to your regular routine as possible. On your Fit List, write down the most important parts of your fitness regimen. But be flexible. If you can't find a stairclimber, join a walking tour. If you can't get to the gym for a yoga class, do some stretches before you climb into bed.

Due to a lack of fitness facilities, time constraints, and too much eating out during a series of business trips, I found myself in terrible shape. I decided to find a personal trainer who could help me create a "road plan," an abbreviated fitness routine that I could do in my hotel. She crafted

TRAVEL LOG

a foolproof, 30-minute, cardio/strength-training combo. I can do it in the morning no matter how early my first meeting. It's not a complete workout, but it's just the ticket for me when I'm on the road.

—*Brian H., Lancaster, Ohio*

Your Medical Picture

Your health is nothing to fool with when you're away from home. Don't assume you'll be able to run to a drugstore for medical items you might need. Fill your regular prescriptions to ensure that you have enough to last the entire trip. Get extra inhalers if you have asthma, or keep a prescription with you in case you run out. Bring any over-the-counter medications you use regularly. And make sure to store your medications in your carry-on bags, not in your checked luggage.

Although it's not something you might want to think about, take the time to prepare for unforeseen problems. Check with your insurance company regarding emergency care outside your coverage area. What information do you need to bring on your trip? Who do you contact if you should fall ill while traveling? If you're going overseas, you may be able to purchase additional coverage for your trip if your policy doesn't already include it. Be sure to keep your emergency information with you at all times.

Getting Your Shots

Knowing what precautions you need to take before an overseas trip takes a little investigation. Many countries require immunizations for international travelers. For the ones that don't, protecting yourself from local health hazards may still mean new shots, boosters, or even medication.

Check with your doctor or a travel clinic about what shots are needed for your destination. The Centers for Disease Control and Prevention (CDC) also has complete lists of immunization requirements, recommended boosters, and medications. It also informs you about common diseases and how best to protect yourself. (See Fitness Resources section.)

Don't wait until the last minute, as some medications must be taken before, during, and after your trip to ensure protection. Plan to get your immunizations well in advance of your trip, as a series of shots may be required for full immunization. The CDC recommends that travelers be vaccinated four to six weeks prior to departure.

IN THE SWIM

If you're a swimmer, you definitely should know about an international directory of pools that are open to the public. The Swimmers Guide Online is a one-of-a-kind resource that lists almost 10,000 pools in 91 countries. (See Resources section.) Every listing includes the name, address, and telephone number of each facility and a description of the pool that includes information on length, number of lanes, water temperature, and whether it is indoors or outdoors. Each listing also gives admission information, including prices for non-members and discounts for senior citizens, those in affiliated groups, and guests at nearby hotels.

YOUR TRAVEL ARRANGEMENTS
Reservations, Please

There are so many things that are out of your control when you travel, make the most of the things you *can* control. Start with reservations. Using your Fit List as a guide, determine the things that you can't possibly live without while traveling, such as a pool, a place to run, or a restaurant with vegetarian fare. Then add those items that would be great but aren't essential, such as bicycle rental or access to tennis courts.

Now, arm yourself with your list and get busy. With the wealth of information available on the Internet, you can reserve a nonsmoking room in a hotel, find out if a restaurant serves organic fare, and even select your seat on a flight. The Internet is a great tool, but it isn't the only one available. Travel guides list hotel facilities as well as places to swim, work out, run, or bike.

Seat Smart

When you reserve your airplane ticket—whether on the Internet or on the telephone—always get a seat assignment. Choosing an aisle seat will make getting up to stretch a lot less of a hassle. Emergency aisle and bulkhead seating usually have more legroom, but book well in advance as these seats fill up fast.

Also consider the time of day you are traveling. An airline's first flight of the morning is most likely to be on time. Midmorning to early afternoon flights are usually less crowded, and if the flight is delayed or canceled there is still time to book another flight and get out the same day.

Call a day or two in advance of your flight to check on how crowded the flight will be. You'll get a good idea of your chances of getting a better seat (next to an empty seat or on an aisle) or upgrading.

No Pie in the Sky

Ask about your options for in-flight meals. While they vary from airline to airline, your choices can include meals for those with special dietary needs (vegetarian, Hindu, kosher, Moslem, Japanese) as well as for those with health-related restrictions (diabetic, gluten-free, bland, soft, low-calorie, low-carbohydrate, low-sodium, low-cholesterol/fat, and sulfite-free).

Don't assume that what will be in a meal will be suitable. Ask specifically what's included in the low-fat or vegetarian meals. Inquire about the use of dairy products and which vegetables, fruits, or meats are served. These are all things you'd want to know about when ordering from a menu at a restaurant, and they should absolutely concern you when you fly.

Order your special meal when you make your flight reservations. Although most airlines say they require only 24-hour's notice, it's best to plan ahead. Reconfirm your meal request at least 48 hours before you leave.

HOW DO AIRPLANE MEALS MEASURE UP?

Whether you're dining on a five-course meal in first class or a chicken-or-beef plate in coach, airplane meals can mean a load of unwanted calories and fat. A recent survey by efit.com, a health-oriented Web site, revealed that airplane meals contain an average of 1,054 calories and 52 grams of fat. According to U.S. Food and Drug Administration recommendations, that's almost a full day's worth of calories and fat in one little meal. Travelers in coach actually fared better than those in the front of the plane. Meals in first class and business class frequently had *more* calories and fat.

Almost all airlines offer special meals that are easier on your waistline. While the quality of ingredients differs from airline to airline, vegetarian meals and fruit or seafood plates are generally good choices for those who are watching their weight. When making reservations, check with the airline about alternative meals. Plan to make your meal selection at this time, mainly to increase your chances of actually getting that meal.

Scope Out Your Options

More and more hotels and chains have Web sites listing the hotel's amenities, including its fitness facility. But no matter where you get your initial information, be specific with your follow-up questions. Use these questions to find out exactly what's available.

▶ The health club. Does the hotel have an in-house gym? What are its hours? Are lockers provided? What kind of equipment is available? (Get brand names if there's a type you prefer.)
▶ Aerobics classes. Are aerobics classes available? At what time? How long is the workout? What is the charge? Is special equipment used?
▶ Swimming pool. Is there a pool? What hours is it open? Are towels provided? How long is the pool in feet or yards? Are there designated lap lanes? Are

kickboards available? Is a bathing cap required? Is there a hot tub? Is there a sauna or steam room? Where are they located?

▶ Videos and television. Does the hotel offer in-room aerobics workouts through the cable television system? If not, are there any early morning aerobics shows on television? Are there workout tapes available to rent? Are there VCRs in the rooms?

▶ Laundry facilities. Is a laundry service available? Is there a coin laundry on the premises or nearby? (If you will be gone for more than a day or two, you need to know how much workout gear to bring.)

▶ Dining options. Check the room service menu. Ask about the nearest vegetarian, organic, and health-oriented restaurants. Find out if there is a health-food store in the neighborhood if you're going to be staying for more than a day or two.

▶ Outdoor activities. Are there running or bicycle trails nearby? What is the route? Is it safe to bike or run alone? Can bicycles be rented at the hotel or nearby? What types of bikes are available? What are the bike rental hours?

If all else fails, ask whether the hotel has any deals with local establishments—a gym, racket club, ski lodge, or golf course—where you can use the facilities at a reduced rate.

FINDING THE "Y"

Your local YMCA or YWCA membership gets you into any facility around the world. You can find the exact location of the Y nearest your destination by using the search feature found on ymca.com. Inputting your destination zip code identifies the Y closest to where you'll be.

Other Options

If your hotel doesn't have a fitness facility, you can still work out. Ask about equipment rentals such as bikes, in-line skates, or even boogie boards. Contact a local sporting goods store about running or biking trails in the area. Your own gym at home may have reciprocal memberships with other clubs around the country. Wouldn't it be nice to know you can walk into a terrific gym just by flashing your membership card? Or call a local chamber of commerce to ask about a dance studio, bowling alley, skating rink, or rock-climbing wall.

WHEN IN ROME

Taking advantage of the local fitness scene wherever you travel can mean anything from skiing to jazz dancing to jogging in a beautiful park. Whatever your destination, finding out how the locals stay fit can be as simple as a click of the mouse. Fodors.com can steer you in the right direction.

The site lets you search for a hotel by the facilities that are available, such as a pool or restaurant. You can also get helpful tips from other visitors to the site. Chamberofcommerce.com lists chambers of commerce and tourism offices around the globe. It highlights each area's top attractions. See Resource section for other Web sites that will keep you in shape.

Room Wise

Once you've scoped out the hotel, it's time to hone in on your room requirements. There are a few basics— air quality, noise, space—that you should consider when reserving a room. Here are some tips for getting what you want, even when money *is* an object.

► Request a nonsmoking room. You won't necessarily get one if you don't ask. The smell of stale smoke in the carpet and upholstery can drive both smokers and nonsmokers to distraction.

► Take noise into account. Rooms near or above hotel lobbies, bars, and restaurants can mean tossing and turning for even the deepest sleepers. Rooms facing a busy street or courtyard pose the same challenge. Top floor rooms are generally the quietest, as there are no overhead footsteps to awaken you from your slumber. Rooms at the ends of hallways and far from the elevators offer the least in the way of noisy hallway traffic. If you're picky, ask your hotel to fax you a floor plan.

▶ Know the size and shape of your room. If you plan to exercise in your room, you've got to have at least a little extra space. Always ask about the dimensions of your room. A room with a full-size bed may have more open floor space than a room with a king-size bed.

▶ Request what matters most to you. If you know you'll want to soak your sore muscles, be sure the room contains a tub. If you need lots of natural light, ask for a south-facing room or a room on an upper floor. Hair dryer, iron, coffeemaker, windows that open to let in the breeze—if you care about these things, make sure they'll be in your room.

▶ Get a written confirmation. Even the best hotels juggle rooms when space gets tight. Get a written confirmation, and bring it with you when you check in.

▶ Complain politely. If your room isn't up to snuff, let the staff known immediately. All of the scouting out and reconfirming you do can't always anticipate a condition or unforeseen circumstance that you might find unacceptable. Ask for the specific room you want firmly but calmly. Ask to speak to a supervisor. Don't take no for an answer, especially if you have a written confirmation.

Meal Plan

Your last task is to check out the local dining scene, both in the hotel and in the surrounding area. If the hotel has one or more restaurants, ask the staff to fax you menus so you can check them out in advance. While you're at it, ask them to fax you menus from any nearby restaurants they recommend. Check out travel guides. Contact local chambers of commerce. If you find a good restaurant, make a reservation in advance. This will leave less to chance (a booked up restaurant won't do you any good no matter how much research you've done) and increase the odds you'll get a terrific meal.

Find out if your hotel room has a small refrigerator or a minibar so you can store healthful snacks and beverages for your stay. You don't need to plan every single thing you're going to eat, but you can stock up on the basics. It'll save you headaches—and those easy acts of self-sabotage—in the long run. You might also find out ahead of time whether there's a good deli or grocery nearby, especially in cities.

You've figured out your basic requirements for planning for a healthy trip. You've used those requirements to make a list of questions to make your plans. You've even made your reservations. Now, let's get packing!

Packing for a Healthy Trip

BEFORE YOU START PACKING, keep in mind something important: Less is more. Packing well doesn't mean filling your bag until the seams burst—it means planning ahead to make the most of the least. Packing—what you pack and how you carry it—is the key to minimizing stress and strain on mind and body.

The general rules for packing hold true for those who want to stay fit and healthy:

- ▶ Pack multifunctional clothes.
- ▶ Wear loose and comfortable clothes for travel days.
- ▶ Pack travel sizes of everything you can.
- ▶ Organize travel kits for toiletries, first aid, and personal documents.
- ▶ Never take anything (clothing or footwear) that you have to break in.

WHAT TO BRING

Before you put the first item in your suitcase, take a look at the lists you made when planning your trip in the first place: your Health and Fitness Requirements and your Fit List. Then peruse the list you made of fitness opportunities at your destination. From those lists you'll be able to decide what you need to pack.

What kind of exercise clothing and equipment will you need while traveling? You've already identified the fitness options that are available where you're going. Look at where you'll be engaging in these activities. Inside or outside? This adds another element to your decision making. If you're headed outside, you must consider climate. Will it be hot and humid or windy and cold? Also consider how long you'll be gone. You may need to pack only one workout outfit if you'll be gone for three days, whereas you'll probably need more if you'll be gone for three weeks.

On Your Feet

A golden rule about shoes is to go with what your feet already know. Take along running or walking shoes that are already well broken in—this is no time to break in new shoes. The same is true for your knocking-around shoes. You might like loafers for shopping at the mall, but after a day's worth of sightseeing they might give you blisters you haven't counted on. If your feet aren't happy, there's not a chance in the world you're going to be.

In the Swim

If swimming is your thing, the packing gods definitely smile on you. All you need is a swimsuit, goggles, a cap, and maybe a pair of flip-flops. Your suit dries easily overnight so you need to bring only one. You can wear a hotel robe or a T-shirt and shorts to the pool. If towels are provided, either from your room or as a poolside amenity, you're all set.

Workout Wear

Plan to bring some version of the workout clothes you usually wear. The key to packing the right clothes is to choose things you can wear more than once and bring only as much as you'll *really* need.

Whatever your workout regimen, you want to avoid cottons and choose instead quick-drying fabrics. You can rinse them out and hang them up and wear them again the same day. Bring two or more pairs of socks so that you can rinse one out and wear the others while the first pair is drying.

Cool Weather Workouts

Layering is important if you'll be exercising outside, especially in colder weather. But now isn't the time to pile on big, puffy layers—no room for that in the suitcase. Instead, bring thin, efficient layers that pack easily and can be peeled off as you work out. To map out what you'll need to pack for a workout outside, remember to bring:

- ▶ Warm hat (such as a stocking cap or an ear-warmer headband)
- ▶ Sunglasses
- ▶ Gloves
- ▶ Long and short-sleeved shirts for layering
- ▶ Nylon windbreaker with pockets for gloves and keys
- ▶ Thermal tights or sweats
- ▶ Undergarments (two sets)
- ▶ Socks (at least two pairs)
- ▶ Running shoes
- ▶ Shoelace ID tag or sport wallet
- ▶ Lip balm and tissues

When the Sun Shines

For warm weather workouts, it's a lot easier to pack light. Planning, however, is no less important. Take along the following:

- ▶ Visor or sunglasses
- ▶ Tank top or short-sleeved shirts
- ▶ Shorts
- ▶ Undergarments (two sets)
- ▶ Socks (at least two pairs)
- ▶ Running shoes
- ▶ Shoelace ID tag or sport wallet
- ▶ Sunscreen
- ▶ Moleskin

Working Out Abroad

It's important to take into account local customs and conditions when you dress for a workout abroad. In many countries revealing clothing is frowned upon, especially for women. To be on the safe side you should dress more conservatively than you might back home. Wear loose-fitting workout clothes that cover your shoulders, stomach, even your arms and legs if the climate allows. A good location-specific guidebook should be able to brief you in advance on local customs.

Exercise Equipment

You *can* take it with you. For portable and packable exercise equipment, consider:

▶ Jump rope. If the ceiling in your hotel room isn't high enough, find a quiet hallway or just go outside.
▶ Resistance bands. These common exercise aids, which are really just large rubber bands, are great for resistance training. They are perfect in a hotel without a gym.
▶ Buoyancy belt. Bring one along to use in the pool. They help in resistance work in the water as well as laps.
▶ Video tapes. Take along your favorite workout tapes. Many hotels have VCRs for use in your room.
▶ Water-filled dumbbells. These are as light as air in your suitcase, but become quite a workout tool when full.

Workout Accessories

Besides the portable exercise gear you can bring on a trip, the important things to pack for a workout are the things you can't do without at home:

▶ Water bottle
▶ Lip balm
▶ Personal stereo

There are some things that you may not always have on hand at home, but will need when you travel. Make sure you bring along a small gym bag and resealable plastic bags for wet swimsuits or dirty clothes.

FITNESS BY MAIL

Specialized mail-order companies such as Magellan's and TravelSmith sell all sorts of travel fitness items. They stock hard-to-find items that will help you keep healthy on the road, such as portable weights, air purifiers, and immune boosters. (See Fitness Resources section.)

Sports Equipment

While most fitness equipment isn't exactly portable, a lot of sports-related equipment is. For instance, if you're going to be near a great golf course, you may want to bring your own clubs. If you'll be at a resort with tennis courts, you won't mind lugging your racket. Here are examples of things to pack for outdoor activities:

▶ Tennis racket, sweatband, and a small towel
▶ Golf clubs, golf shoes, and a supply of golf balls
▶ Swim cap, goggles, earplugs
▶ Bike helmet and water bottle
▶ In-line skates, helmet, and pads

Portable Edibles

What you bring along on your travels depends on your mode of transport. If you're driving, you can pack a cooler full of healthy things to snack on. Favorite car snacks include:

- ► Bite-size pieces of vegetables
- ► Bottled water
- ► Energy bars
- ► Fruit
- ► Pretzels or whole wheat crackers
- ► Raisins
- ► Rice cakes
- ► Salads
- ► Sandwiches
- ► Trail mix

Food on the Fly

Saying no to food on planes and in airports is often a good idea because it gives you more control over what goes into your body. But that means bringing along your own munchies. Carry enough for the whole trip, including any unexpected delays, so that you won't be tempted to reach for that second or third bag of peanuts.

Any of the above-noted snacks are appropriate take-alongs for plane travel (as well as for car or train travel). Just be sure to pack food in tightly sealed plastic bags or containers and store it in an insulated tote if it is perishable. Bring napkins, plastic utensils, and bottled water so you don't have to be at the mercy of the flight attendants.

Bringing a snack for a short flight is easy. It's tougher, however, to pack a meal for a longer flight because of limited space. Here are a few ideas on what to bring from home:

▶ The smaller, the better. Bring individual servings of what you'll eat most. Packets of low-fat salad dressing, individual cans of tuna, and serving-size packages of crackers tuck easily into your carry-on.
▶ Cool carry-ons. Carry uncrushable, unbruisable items with you, such as protein bars, boxes of raisins, and bottles of water.
▶ Portable potables. If you are packing food for the duration of your stay, bring only the most portable of potables, such as tea bags, instant soup, cereal bars, and single-serving packages of cereal.
▶ Liquid rules. Don't pack juice boxes in your checked luggage, as they're likely to blow up in the nonpressurized baggage compartment. You usually don't need to pack extra bottles of water because you can just refill the one you bring on board as many times as you like.
▶ Mess kits. Bring paper napkins, plastic utensils, and disposable plates.

Your Health Records

If you have any health-related conditions that a medical team should know about in the case of an emergency, make sure this information is readily accessible. Many people choose to wear a bracelet listing any medical conditions. Others bring along documentation from their physicians. Make copies of pertinent records and store them in waterproof plastic you keep with you at all times. You might create a laminated card that you keep with your identification, which notes:

▶ Medical conditions, such as high blood pressure, diabetes, or the presence of a pacemaker.

▶ All allergies, from antibiotics to peanut butter to the adhesive used in many bandage materials.

▶ Any special requirements, such as procedures dictated by your insurance company in order to make sure your treatment is covered.

Your Medications

Keep all your prescription medications in their original containers. This will help to make procedure through customs go more smoothly. As a precaution, take copies of your prescriptions with you. If you take narcotics for medical reasons and are traveling abroad, get a letter from your doctor explaining your need for this medicine in case there is any question in customs. Bring any over-the-counter medications, such as sleep aids or motion-sickness pills, you might need. This is especially important for any travel outside of the United States, as some medicines are difficult to buy in other countries. And don't forget eyedrops and a spare pair of glasses or contact lenses.

You don't need to carry full packages of all of these items. Invest in a pillbox with plenty of compartments

---

TRAVEL LOG

Air travel sets my sinuses off with sneezing and congestion. On a recent trip to Hawaii, I was a sneezy, miserable mess for the entire five-hour flight, much to the chagrin of my fellow passengers. When I got off the plane, I paid something like $20 for a travel-size package of cold medicine and a miniature bottle of nasal spray at the airport shop. What a chump! Now I take precautionary medication before I board the plane and pack plenty of extra (and reasonably priced) stuff—just in case.

—Kathy R., Davis, California

---

so you can carry only what you need. Use travel sizes whenever possible, or pack small quantities in marked and dated resealable plastic bags.

First Aid Kits

Your medicine cabinet won't be within reach when you're traveling, so make sure you have medications you might need in case of emergency. It's a good idea to put together a compact first aid kit. Pack it with items you might need if you catch a cold or get minor burns or cuts. And don't forget treatments for maladies many travelers encounter, such as indigestion or blisters.

FIRST AID KIT CHECKLIST

- ☐ Antacids, laxatives, and diarrhea medicines
- ☐ Antibiotic ointments
- ☐ Bandages
- ☐ Cold medicine
- ☐ Cortisone cream
- ☐ Moleskin for blisters
- ☐ Nasal spray
- ☐ Pain relievers such as aspirin, ibuprofen, or acetaminophen
- ☐ Scissors
- ☐ Tweezers

Smart Luggage

There are all shapes and sizes of luggage, some designed for looks and some designed for lugging. You want to look for the latter kind, and you want the kind that works with your body, not against it. Traveling healthy means having a bag that won't rip your rotator cuff, strain your lower back, or cause other injuries. Choose bags that are kind to your body.

Luggage design has come a long way. Remember those suitcases that had wheels on the bottom and a little loop of a handle? You had to stoop over just to drag them along, and sometimes they just toppled over for no reason. The designers finally created bags that actually work. The telescoping handle of the vertical Pullman rises from the top and is high enough for you to be able to stand up straight while pulling it along on sturdy wheels. You can even place your carry-on bag on top and drag that along as well. The best part is that these bags put less strain on your back and shoulders than any other type of luggage. There's no good reason why you shouldn't consider this type of bag.

The Duffel Deal

A duffel bag is great for portability. It's pliable and fairly easy to carry by hand or over the shoulder—if it's not packed to bursting and threatening to knock you over with every step. Just because it's big and can hold a lot doesn't mean you have to fill it up. If possible, go for the duffel with wheels, which can be dragged by the opposite corner. More expensive models can be pulled by a telescoping handle.

Hang It Up

Garment bags are for people traveling with clothing that needs special attention, such as a business traveler who needs to bring a suit or a cruise ship passenger who needs a few dressy outfits. They're good at keeping suits and formal clothing looking nice, but they're in a class by themselves carrying-wise. When folded in half, they can be bulky and unwieldy; and carrying them when they hang long is like carrying a big batch of hanging clothes home from the dry cleaners. Make sure you don't overpack a garment bag, and then be sure to balance it with a bag on the other side. That way you limit the strain to your body.

Back It Up

Backpacks are great for casual travel and ideal for children. The weight is evenly balanced and your hands are free to deal with children or tickets or whatever. But no matter how convenient this type of bag, if you overpack it the strain on your shoulders can be excruciating. If you're thinking about traveling with a backpack, try on several styles and walk around with them before you buy. If you're not comfortable with an empty pack, you'll be in tears when it's full.

PACKING PARTICULARS

Packing your bags to minimize strain takes some thought. How do you pack to make your bags more manageable? First, pack as lightly as you can. Second, pack well in advance of your trip. Take a practice walk with your bags around the house to be sure you can manage the load. If you have to repack, you'll have plenty of time to do so. If you have to pack things in the outside compartments of your bag, be sure you can still carry your bag comfortably. If it's bumpy and awkward to carry, repack it.

An important measure of whether you've bitten off more than you can chew is the Lift Test. If you can't pick your bag up over your head (as if you're about to try to stow it in an overhead bin) or carry it up a flight of stairs, then it's too heavy. Rethink your packing strategy. If you can't lighten your load, consider dividing your gear among two or more bags or rent a cart at the airport to haul the baggage through check-in.

Carry-on Capers

Carry-on bags are the real thorn in a traveler's side. The problem is that carry-ons such as briefcases, handbags, and laptops have shoulder straps. These create shoulder strain that often lingers long after you've gotten home. Switching to a wheeled carry-on option, or a backpack that distributes weight evenly between your shoulders, will eliminate that condition.

Pack things you'll need easy access to in a carry-on that you can stow under the seat in front of you:

▶ Water bottle
▶ Snacks
▶ Reading material
▶ Personal stereo
▶ Saline spray
▶ Lip balm
▶ Sleep mask
▶ Slippers or socks
▶ Small toiletries kit—toothbrush, toothpaste, hairbrush, and moisturizing lotion

Pack things you won't need immediately in another bag to put in the overhead bin:

▶ Full toiletries kit
▶ Workout gear
▶ Change of clothes
▶ Camera and film
▶ Personal documents kit

If you're going to keep your carry-on luggage under the seat, make sure you haven't packed so much that you'll have to squash the contents to make it fit. Another good

YOUR TOILETRY KIT

A well-packed toiletry kit for any fitness-minded traveler includes:

- ☐ Antibacterial wipes
- ☐ Bath soap
- ☐ Bottle opener
- ☐ Cologne or perfume
- ☐ Comb and brush
- ☐ Corkscrew
- ☐ Cotton swabs
- ☐ Dental floss
- ☐ Deodorant
- ☐ Eyeglass repair kit
- ☐ Facial cleanser
- ☐ Hair conditioner
- ☐ Hair styling products
- ☐ Hand lotion
- ☐ Insect repellent
- ☐ Laundry detergent
- ☐ Lip balm
- ☐ Makeup
- ☐ Matches
- ☐ Moisturizer
- ☐ Mouthwash
- ☐ Nail clippers
- ☐ Nail file
- ☐ Nail polish remover
- ☐ Razor
- ☐ Small screw-driver
- ☐ Sewing kit
- ☐ Shampoo
- ☐ Shaving cream
- ☐ Sunscreen
- ☐ Swiss Army knife
- ☐ Tissues
- ☐ Toothbrush
- ☐ Toothpaste
- ☐ Tweezers

reason to keep your carry-on slim is that some airports now have templates at security checks. If your bag doesn't fit through, you'll be asked to check it.

TRAVEL LOG

On a recent trip to Chicago, I realized I had become the kind of traveler I had once stared at in disgust. I was struggling with hideously oversized and overpacked luggage that looked like two 80-pound punching bags hanging from shoulder straps. I had become a pack mule, carrying everything the kids might want or need. I'm a born-again light traveler now, back down to a single bag packed with no more than two pairs of shoes, a versatile combination of black and gray clothing, and smart, spare little kits for toiletries. And my kids are now in charge of hauling their own stuff!

—*Marylise C., Fairfield, Connecticut*

RELAXATION AND WELL-BEING

One of the tricks to staying cool when traveling is to keep yourself as comfortable and relaxed as possible. This takes planning both for travel time and at your destination. These items can soothe mind and body and entertain your brain:

▶ A portable white-noise machine
▶ A book
▶ Personal stereo and tapes or CDs
▶ Earplugs
▶ Eyeshades
▶ Inflatable pillow
▶ Lip balm
▶ Moisturizer
▶ Pillowcase
▶ Slippers or thick socks

Reading light

Many people look forward to using their travel time—in transit or during their stay—to catch up on reading or indulge in some extra pleasure reading. This is indeed one of the true upsides of travel, but it's important to pack smart when it comes to reading material. Don't

Every time I travel, I take along articles torn from dozens of magazines, the ones I just can't seem to stay ahead of in my regular life (picture a stack of *New Yorker* magazines gathering dust on my bedside table). I relish

TRAVEL LOG

the opportunity to catch up on this pure-pleasure reading, and it helps make for a very relaxing ride. Best of all, I can discard the articles when I'm done. And my carry-on is much lighter for my return flight. How often can you say that?

—Carole T., Shaker Heights, Ohio

get stuck hauling a bunch of books or magazines you might not get a chance to read:

Bring paperbacks, not hardcovers

It's tempting to bring the latest best-seller, but wait until it comes out in paperback. It's hard to find the motivation to carry a heavy hardcover book you've just finished all the way home.

Leave finished books behind

Small hotels and rental accommodations often accumulate a library of left-behind books—a welcome sight if you've run out of appealing things to read. Think of it as sharing your love of reading and lightening your load as you go.

Don't overreach

That weekend at the beach might not be the best time to tackle the complete works of Tolstoy. Create your reading list based on the kinds of books and magazines you read at home.

Two-for-one plan

If you're traveling with a companion, bring books and magazines you'll both read to cut the ballast of reading material in half.

Inspirational words

Pack a health book or magazine to keep you motivated to exercise and eat right. *This* works.

Packing the Sheep

Getting a good night's sleep on the road can be difficult. Noise is among the biggest factors. Ever lie awake in a hotel room listening to noisy neighbors, banging elevator doors, or hallway conversation? A simple fix is to take along some earplugs. If you're a frequent traveler, invest in a travel-size ambient noise machine, which creates a soothing, white noise that blocks out other aggravating sounds.

Another problem when traveling is that the hotel is just not your home. You miss your bed, your pillow. So bring your favorite pajamas to help you relax. Pack one of your own pillowcases to remind you of home. Tuck a night-light in your bag so you won't stub your toe on your way to the bathroom in the middle of the night. Perhaps a scented candle is the final touch that will turn your hotel room into a cozy nesting spot and allow you the restful sleep you need to stay energetic during the day.

3

Before You Leave Home

THINK ABOUT THE LAST TRIP you took. Before you left you were probably rushing around to get everything ready, working late to tie up loose ends at the office, and making sure the pets would be fed and the plants watered. Then you had to dash to the airport and just barely made your flight.

You were exhausted before the plane left the ground. This is *not* the best way to start your trip.

An important part of healthy travel is taking care of yourself before you leave. Don't let last minute details interfere with your regular healthful routine. Get enough sleep and eat right. Your body is going to take enough abuse on the road. Make sure you're ready to travel—in mind and body.

WHERE DOES THE TIME GO?

You ditch your aerobics class the night before a trip because you still have to pack. Or on the way home from work, you stop for a cheeseburger and fries at the drive-through because you didn't have time for lunch. Does this sound familiar? Try to stick with your healthful routine even when you are sweating the small stuff. This is the time to eat right and exercise.

Exercising Beforehand

You should always plan to exercise before you travel. Besides the obvious physical benefits, exercising before a trip has strong psychological advantages as well. When you feel like you've been doing right by your body by exercising, you're less likely to abandon your program when you're on the road. Think of it as shoring up your resolve before you hit the road. If you let your exercise schedule slip before you travel, you're more likely to fall into an all-or-nothing attitude that makes it easy to justify putting fitness on hold when you travel.

Make yourself a schedule, mapping out all the things you have to do before you leave, including exercise. Your most immediate pre-trip workout should be the night before if you're traveling in the morning, and in the morning if you're traveling later in the day. At the very least, get up a half an hour early the day you leave to fit in a brisk walk. The point is to get your blood moving and to get oxygen to all points of your body.

On the days leading up to your trip, be conscientious about maintaining your workout schedule. If you just can't manage this, don't try to compensate with a blowout workout before you leave. Just do some stretching or yoga instead. You don't want sore muscles for traveling, and a big workout at night can interfere with your sleep.

Getting There in Time

If you're flying, try to get to the airport with plenty of time to spare. Airlines recommend that you arrive at least one hour in advance for a domestic flight and two hours in advance for international travel. Sticking to this schedule will safeguard your travel arrangements because you're there, checked in, and ready at the gate. If you're late anything can happen, including having your seat handed off to a standby passenger. In addition, the extra time you allow yourself will give you a chance to prepare yourself for the flight both mentally and physically. There's more to getting ready to fly than just checking your bags. You're going to be cooped up on a plane for a while, so give yourself some prep time.

EXERCISE BEFORE YOU BOARD

You've got plenty of time before your flight leaves. Rather than dropping by the airport bar for a quick beer, opt for exercise. Take a couple of minutes to stretch or take a 10-minute walk. Before you even get on the plane, you're trying to keep your energy up and your body revved for travel.

The Long Walk

The easiest way to exercise at the airport is to go for a walk. Just look at the map of most larger airports and you'll see a sprawling layout of concourses and terminals. Even smaller airports have room for walking. Take a 10 to 15-minute walk before you board and follow up with bit of stretching in an uncrowded part of the airport, such as an unused waiting area. Walking improves blood circulation, which can help to minimize leg cramping from the close quarters on the plane.

If you don't have a traveling companion who can watch your bags while you do your fitness walk, head for the lockers. You'll find them in many terminals and they cost just a couple of bucks.

Preboarding Stretches

Stretching is just as important as walking before boarding. You're going to be confined to a cramped space on the plane, so take advantage of the wide-open terminal while you can. Find a quiet place and start stretching.

To improve circulation in your legs and stretch the calves, you can stretch while sitting or standing. (If you're standing, make sure to lean against something like a wall or a chair for support.) Lift your right knee and rotate your foot in a circle to the left 8 to 10 times. Then rotate to the right 8 to 10 times. Then try to slowly write the letters of the alphabet using your foot as a pencil. Go all out and try both upper- and lowercase letters. Switch sides and repeat one more time through.

To stretch your thighs, knees, and ankles, start by standing up straight, using your right hand to balance yourself. Bending at the knees, lift your right foot behind you and grab the top of your right foot with your left hand. Slowly pull your heel toward your backside as you straighten your standing leg until you feel a stretch. Hold this position for 10 to 20 seconds. Repeat with the other leg. Do this a total of five times per side.

For the back of the thigh and lower back, cross your right foot over your left and bend at the waist with your arms and head hanging down like a rag doll. Make sure your neck is relaxed. Hold for 10 seconds and pull your body slowly and gently back to an upright position. Switch legs and repeat. Once or twice is plenty.

This back exercise can be done while standing in the check-in line. (Be sure to put your bags down first.) Stand with your hands on your hips, feet shoulder distance apart, knees slightly bent. Gently turn your upper body toward the right, keeping your hips stationary, and look over your right shoulder. Hold for 10 seconds. Breathe normally as you hold the stretch. Switch to the left side and repeat. Do four sets of this stretch.

The easiest, most effective way to stretch your neck is to do neck rotations. Standing or sitting up straight, slowly drop your head toward your right shoulder. Rotate your head around the front to the left shoulder, then come back to an upright position. If you have neck problems, you should skip this exercise. Do this five times slowly.

To stretch your shoulders, just shrug. Lift your shoulders upward toward your ears until you feel a slight tension. Hold for five seconds, then let your shoulders drop to a natural position. Repeat three times. For an added kick, shrug your shoulders and rotate them, one at time, forward for five rotations. Shrug again and rotate them backward. If you have shoulder problems, don't bother with this stretch.

EATING BEFORE DEPARTURE

What you eat in the days before you travel is significant. In a best case scenario, you're working to beef up your body's natural defenses. Choose well-balanced meals, including foods such as carrots, cabbage, cauliflower, garlic, and peppers to charge up the immune system. Don't neglect whole grains and leafy vegetables, which contain beneficial antioxidants.

Avoid sugary and fatty foods before a trip, as they can make you jumpy or sluggish. Lay off caffeine and alcohol. These act as diuretics and will leave you dehydrated. Drink water in place of coffee, tea, or alcoholic beverages.

Be aware that whatever you eat the night before traveling can affect your mood the next day. Eat a balanced dinner (vegetables, protein, and whole grains) the night before, but early in the evening to give your body plenty of time to digest it. If you're nervous or keyed up about traveling, eat something that will help you sleep. Foods containing the amino acid tryptophan— turkey, milk, and bananas—can help you relax.

Home, Eat Home

Eating the day you actually travel should follow one simple rule—don't get on the plane hungry. The reason is that your food choices on a flight are limited to what the airline chooses to serve you. We all know the regular airplane meals don't have your best interests at heart. If you packed healthy snacks for the flight, great. But if you don't eat before you board or don't bring along healthy snacks, you're just a diet disaster waiting to happen. If you're ravenous, you'll probably be reaching for every bag of peanuts you can get your hands on.

Even if you have an early morning flight, eat a light breakfast. And as baseball legend Satchel Paige once said, "Avoid greasy meats as they angry up the blood." That goes double at 30,000 feet. Stick with a protein source such as skim milk, cheese, or yogurt and pair it with fruit and a whole-grain cereal, toast, or bagel. Snag a granola bar if that's all you have time for, but eat enough to hold you over until your next meal or snack.

My favorite pretravel breakfast, refined after something like a half million miles of business travel, is an egg-white omelette with double spinach, cooked without oil or butter if possible. Add a side of whole wheat toast and a dollop of

TRAVEL LOG

Dijon mustard for tang. Top it off with a cup of herbal tea and lemon and you've given your body the gift of a perfect mix of protein and carbs, minus fat, which can upset your system throughout a day of flying.

—*Oren G., Buffalo, New York*

If you have an afternoon flight, stick with the same plan. A sandwich with lean meat and tomato and lettuce on whole-grain bread should keep your hunger at bay. Include a glass of milk or a container of yogurt for extra protein.

TAKE YOUR VITAMINS

Before you board an airplane, try loading up on vitamins C and E and the mineral zinc. Experts believe they boost your immune system and fight infections. The herb echinacea also has a reputation for preventing or reducing symptoms of colds. Check with you doctor about these vitamin, mineral, and herb supplements.

THE IN-FLIGHT CLIMATE

The air in the cabin of a plane is notoriously dry. The humidity can be as low as 2 percent, as compared to a usual comfort level of 50 percent. When you consider you'll be enduring this for some length of time, the big problem is dehydration. The answer? Water, water, and more water.

Prepare yourself by drinking plenty of water before you even get on the plane. Dehydration—when your body loses too much water—sets in even before you feel thirsty or experience telltale symptoms such as a dry mouth or sticky saliva. That's why it's important to constantly drink water, thirsty or not. And don't count on the flight attendants—bring along your own water bottle.

Flying With a Cold

It's not a good idea to travel if you're ill, but sometimes your travel plans can't be changed. The cabin pressure

I have a very strict policy of drinking twice as much water as usual on days that I fly. I'm usually a two-liter-a-day person, so getting in twice that can be a challenge. But it's worth it. I don't feel as bloated and gassy when I get off the plane as I used to, my

TRAVEL LOG

skin feels better, and it helps me get a good night's sleep. One tip, though. Book an aisle seat so you can get to the bathroom without disrupting your seatmates.

—*Ellen W., Cranston, Rhode Island*

and the dry air in a plane exaggerate cold symptoms, so take these precautions to help minimize the effects:

▶ Take a nasal decongestant tablet or use a spray a half hour before flight time to help relieve pressure in the sinuses and ears during takeoff.

▶ Drink lots of water to help thin out the mucus and relieve congestion.

▶ Yawn or swallow frequently during the flight, especially during takeoff and landing to equalize pressure in the ears. Chew gum or suck on hard candy to make you swallow more often.

▶ If swallowing doesn't work, try the "Valsalva maneuver." Pinch your nostrils shut with your thumb and index finger. Gently force air to the back of the nose—as if you're trying to blow you fingers off your nostrils. Do this in short, gentle blasts until you feel your ears pop.

As a last resort, you can try taking the warm cloths flight attendants hand out for washing your hands and holding them over your ears. The steam can help equalize the pressure. It looks silly, but it may work for you.

The Eyes Have It

Don't forget about your eyes when preparing for cabin dryness. Your eyes will feel the effects of the lack of humidity as much as the rest of your body. If you usually wear contact lenses, consider wearing glasses on the plane. Bring eyedrops or saline solution and use them once every hour. If you plan to sleep on the plane, it's better to remove contacts before dozing off.

Be Kind to Your Skin

The drying effects of the air can wreak havoc on your skin. Washing your hands frequently (which you should do to kill virulent germs found in the closed environment on planes) can also exacerbate the situation. Use moisturizers on your hands and face before you board and as necessary throughout the flight. Try to apply hand lotion when your hands are a bit damp. Prep with lip balm to combat dry, chapped lips. Also, wear clothes made from cotton instead of synthetics, as cotton breathes better and keeps you more comfortable.

Cabin Concerns

In-flight climate isn't only about dry air. The air pressure in the cabin of a plane is normally stabilized at 8,000 feet above sea level—akin to the altitude in the Rocky Mountains. Combined with the air pressure, sitting for long periods of time can cause edema, or swelling of the extremities. To feel more comfortable, wear loose-fitting clothing. Opt for shoes you can loosen up and that won't restrict the blood flow to your feet. Or you can bring along an extra pair of socks to wear on the plane so you can slip off your shoes to improve circulation. If you wear tight-fitting jewelry, including rings, take it off until you've arrived at your destination.

COMBAT JET LAG

Jet lag can occur when you cross two or more time zones in a short period of time. When you land, clocks display local time, but your body's internal clock is still tuned to back home time. Symptoms can include fatigue, inability to fall asleep or to stay awake, lack of appetite, intestinal discomforts, and disorientation, to name a few. Experts say that it takes the body at least a day to recover for every time zone crossed. That means if you fly from California to New York, it could take three days for your body to return to normal. A transatlantic flight requires even more recovery time.

Your first defense against jet lag is a healthy lifestyle. A well-balanced diet and regular exercise strengthen your body and make it easier to bounce back from jet lag. But there are more specific things you can do as well.

The Time Factor

Many experts who study the effects of jet lag agree that setting your watch for your destination's time zone will help you mentally adjust to the time change. You can even begin to live by the new time zone before you leave home. Start changing your sleeping and eating patterns to your destination time. This can be difficult to achieve if you live in a full house with everyone else on home time, but it's worth a try.

Curtail Alcohol and Caffeine

Steer clear of alcohol and caffeine before and during your flight. Both leave you dehydrated, which exacerbates the symptoms of jet lag. Both also disrupt your sleep, leaving you tired the next day.

Don't Overeat

Avoid the big meals many airlines serve on long flights. Overeating makes you sluggish and sleepy, thus making you more tired when you arrive.

Try Melatonin

Doctors believe the over-the-counter drug melatonin helps the body reset its internal clock. Studies indicate that melatonin helps travelers become accustomed to a new time zone more quickly.

Get Some Sun

Studies have shown that simply getting some sun when you arrive can help you adjust to a new time zone.

Feasting and Fasting to Beat Jet Lag

You can try a special pretravel diet, like the one developed by Dr. Charles F. Ephet of the Argonne National Laboratory in Illinois (a research facility for the U.S. Department of Energy). This method of relieving jet lag calls for a combination of feasting and fasting for three days before you travel. This diet is designed to change your biological clock through adjusting the levels of glycogen (the main store of the body's energy) and xanthines (a class of chemicals including caffeine) in your body through eating more and less of certain foods at specific times of the day.

No matter what direction you are flying—from California to Europe, from New York to Hawaii—follow the three-day directions below. Then, depending on whether your trip is toward the east or toward the west, apply the appropriate travel-day routine.

Day one

Eat 35 percent more calories than usual. For breakfast and lunch, make sure your meal is high in protein, low in carbohydrates. Dinner should be a high-carbohydrate meal. Have caffeine only in the afternoon. Go to bed at your regular time.

Day two

Take in a fraction of the calories consumed the day before—no more than 800 calories. Breakfast and lunch should be high in protein, dinner high in carbohydrates. Restrict caffeine to the afternoon. Go to bed at your regular time.

Day three

Follow the dietary guidelines for Day One. Stay up past your normal bedtime.

Travel day (flying west)

If possible, sleep in a little. If you drink coffee, have two or three cups in the morning, then avoid caffeine for the rest of the day. Eat a low-calorie, high-protein breakfast, then try to avoid eating until breakfast time in your destination.

If your flight does not leave until late in the day, keep daytime activities to a minimum—just light exercise and stretching. If it will be daytime when you arrive at your destination, try to sleep on the plane. Use a mask to block out light and earplugs to block noise. If it will be nighttime when you arrive, try to stay awake so you can sleep when you reach your destination.

Travel day (flying east)

Get up as early as possible and eat as little as possible, avoiding caffeine. Stay active in the early part of the day. At about 6 PM, set your watch to destination time. Try to sleep on the flight until it is breakfast time at your destination.

Treat the day you arrive as a feast day, avoiding caffeine and getting to bed on time. The following day, eat a high-protein breakfast and resume a normal schedule. Resist the urge to sleep in the middle of the day.

4

En Route

WHAT YOU DO TO KEEP YOURSELF FIT and healthy while you travel will affect how you feel when you arrive. Whether it's an 18-hour flight or a half-day car trip, you should use time wisely during transit. To arrive refreshed and ready to go, try some of these tips.

GETTING SETTLED

When you board an airplane, you have to negotiate down the narrow aisle as you find your seat. Most people contort their body to try to avoid bopping another passenger in the head with a bag. This is a sure way to injure your back. But there are some easy ways to maneuver the aisle without hurting anyone—yourself included. The trick is to position your bags—briefcases, laptops, purses—so that you can manage them easily and comfortably.

In the front-to-back maneuver, you keep your shoulders, torso, and hips facing forward. Carry your bags in front and behind you with both your wrists facing your body (reversing your grip on the bag behind you will cause your torso to twist). Your heavier bag should be in front of you. The lighter bag will be easier to manage behind you, as the triceps muscles you're using to carry the one in back are usually less developed than the biceps carrying the one in front.

For the side slide, find out which side of the plane you're seated on when you board. Then position your body so you are facing that side of the aisle. Keep your shoulders, torso, and hips facing the seats, bags in both hands to your sides. Turn your head to look down the aisle to see where you're going, but keep your body parallel to the seats. Sidestep your way down the aisle to your seat. If you're wearing a back-pack, make sure you aren't hitting everyone in the face along the way.

Bags and Bins

Stowing your carry-on luggage is among your first challenges in getting settled. Should your bags go in the overhead bin or under the seat in front of you? Make sure you've got the essentials in a bag under the seat in front of you so you won't need to open the overhead bin once you're underway. The scowling disapproval of fellow passengers whom you have to crawl over isn't the only problem. You also want to avoid having to handle heavy bags more than necessary.

When stowing your bag overhead, remember to:

▶ Give yourself enough room to maneuver in the aisle. You can't get into the proper position if someone is trying to squeeze behind you.
▶ Spread your feet about shoulders-width apart and bend your knees slightly when lifting a heavy bag.
▶ Try to keep your shoulders in line over your hips when lifting. This helps stop you from leaning backward to reach the bin. Besides being uncomfortable, it puts too much pressure on your back.

Finally, ask for assistance from the flight attendant if you can't manage the bag yourself. There's no surer way to throw out your back than lifting a bag that is too heavy or bulky. Your back will thank you for it.

Have a Seat

Before you take a seat, do a few stretches—some neck rolls, shoulder rolls, and a quick stretch or two with your arms over your head. Rotate your torso gently side to side to stretch your back. And don't forget to take some deep breaths to release tension.

The problem with most airline seats is that they don't give enough support for your spine. You see people contorted into all sorts of positions in an effort to get comfortable. It *can* be done, however. When you sit down, tilt your pelvis forward a little until you feel your upper body lift forward from the back of the seat. Your spine is curved in its natural position with your shoulders back and your chest out. This position will keep you feeling more relaxed.

Unfortunately, most airplane seats are designed to keep you slumped. Your spine curves outward toward the back of the chair and your shoulders and chest slump forward. This position puts extra strain on your body. You'll be feeling the strain in no time.

To make sure you're sitting in the proper position, slide back in the seat as far as you can. Place an airline pillow, a rolled-up towel, or a folded sweater in the small of your back, fitting it in the natural curve of your spine. Place another one behind your neck. Varying your leg positions will also help circulation. Stretch them out in front of you for a minute or two, flex your feet, or even lift your knee toward your chest. Try propping them up on a book or a bag under your seat. Don't cross your legs, as this can restrict blood flow to the calves and create potentially serious blood clots in the legs on longer flights.

ECONOMY-CLASS SYNDROME

"Economy-class syndrome" may sound a bad joke, but it's a very real and serious medical condition. On flights of four hours or more, the combination of cramped quarters, dry and pressurized cabins, dehydration, and long periods of inactivity can restrict blood flow and cause blood clots in the legs. These can break free and travel to the lungs, where they can block the flow of blood. In very rare cases this condition can be fatal.

Some people appear to suffer more often this condition: smokers, heavy drinkers, the elderly, and people with existing heart conditions. People who fly frequently are also at greater risk. The symptoms, which include chest pain and coughing, may not appear for days after travel, so diagnosis is difficult.

You can lower your risk in a number of ways:

▶ If you can tolerate aspirin, take one a day for a few days before you travel. It can help prevent clots from forming. Remember to check with your doctor first.
▶ Wear loose clothing and footwear.
▶ Before you board, massage your calves and thighs and move your ankles in a circular motion to increase blood flow. Continue to do this every half hour or so during the flight.
▶ Get up and move around the cabin. Simple movement and stretching every hour keeps the blood circulating.

EXERCISE IN THE AIR

Believe it or not, the confined space of an airplane is a great place to exercise. It allows you to isolate specific muscles to get a natural resistance-type workout. Basic stretches as well as specialized yoga routines also are easy to modify for air travel.

Muscle-Isolation Exercises

Isometric tightening of the muscles is the simplest—most inconspicuous—way to exercise on board. This technique uses very small movements, so you can exercise while watching the in-flight movie or reading a book and no one will be the wiser. Isometric tightening works for lots of different areas of the body: thighs, stomach, shoulder, upper back, and arms. First, choose a muscle or group of muscles, such as your stomach muscles. Sit up straight and take a deep breath. As you exhale, tighten your stomach muscles and hold for a count of 10. Release and breathe in. Do this 5 to 10 times. Choose a different muscle group to work on every 20 minutes or so. Don't forget to cool down with deep breaths and stretches when you're finished.

Legs

Sit up straight with your feet flat on the floor, if possible. Keeping your knee bent, raise your right leg a few inches off the floor. Rotate the foot around a circle to the right eight times, then reverse the motion. Do the same with the left leg. Repeat five times.

Shoulders

For the shoulders and arms, start with shrugs. While breathing in, pull your shoulders up toward your ears and hold for a count of 10. Breathe out and release. Repeat five times.

Biceps

This standard exercise is done this time using your body's natural resistance instead of weights. Lower your arms to your sides and make fists. Tighten your biceps, breathe in, and slowly raise your fists toward your shoulders. Breathe out and slowly lower your fists to the starting position. Do this 10 times. Keep the muscles tight and control the movements going both up and down.

Triceps

This is an exercise that uses your armrests, so try it if both are available and they're of a sturdy, stable design. With your feet planted firmly on the ground, place your hands on the ends of your armrests, palms down. Breathe in and lift yourself up out of your seat. Don't let your elbows lock when your arms are extended. Exhale and lower yourself an inch or two, but don't actually touch the seat. Repeat five to seven times.

Stretching En Route

Stretching is one of the easiest ways to keep moving while in the air. Just getting up out of your seat stretches your legs. It keeps your blood circulating and warms up muscles that have stiffened from sitting. Stand in the aisle or the back of the plane to give yourself some room. Following are some simple stretches and exercises that are perfect for a cramped space.

Lower body stretches

Grasp the back of a seat or lean against a wall for balance. To stretch out your hamstrings and calves, place one leg behind you about 12 inches from your front heel. Shift your weight to the back leg and bend the knee slightly. Slowly lean forward (keeping your back straight) over the front foot to stretch the hamstring. Repeat with the other side. For your calves, in the same starting position as the hamstring stretch, bend your front leg at the knee this time and shift your weight forward over the bent knee and you'll feel your calf muscles stretch. Switch legs and repeat.

Upper body stretches

To stretch your back, place your hands on your hips (or keep them at your side, if space isn't available) and twist your shoulders and torso slowly from side to side. To relax tight shoulder muscles, interlace your fingers together behind your back, palms facing your body, arms relaxed. Slowly straighten your arms and pull your shoulder blades together until you feel a stretch. Hold for a count of 10. For both shoulders and arms, draw your right arm across your chest toward the left and parallel to the floor. With your left arm, push your right arm at the elbow as close to your body as possible. Hold this for a count of 10 and repeat with the other side.

Sitting stretches

When you're confined to your seat because of a "Fasten Seat Belt" sign, you can do the same stretches for your neck and shoulders described above. Just scoot up a little toward the edge of the cushion.

The lower body is a bit more difficult because you've got very limited space. If you can, move what's under the seat in front of you so you have some room to maneuver. Start by extending your legs as far as they will go. Point your toes toward the floor, then flex them back toward your body. Do this several times during the trip—at least once an hour if you haven't been able to leave your seat. This will not only stretch your calf muscles, but it will increase the blood circulation in your legs. Next, start with both feet flat on the floor. Lift up your heels and hold that position for 10 seconds. Return your heels to the floor and then lift your toes and hold for 10 seconds.

One of the best ways to stretch your back in such a confined space is to lean forward and over your knees, keeping your chin tucked to your chest. Your arms should be relaxed and hanging next to your calves. If you can't bend all the way without bumping your head, just bend as far as you can. When you pull yourself up, elongate your spine by slowly raising your head from your chest and sitting up as straight as possible. After that, push your shoulders forward and pull in your stomach. Release and push your shoulders back and arch your back slightly. Repeat slowly a few times and you'll feel the center of your back loosen.

Airplane Yoga

You've done straightforward exercises and stretches—now try some yoga. The point of yoga is to bring the mind, body, and spirit into alignment through ancient *asanas*—the traditional stretches or positions. In the cramped quarters of a plane, these positions can reduce muscle tension through stretching and deep breathing.

Open chest stretch

Sit toward the edge of your seat with your hands holding onto the sides of the cushion. Slowly lift your chest up and forward. Open your chest out by bringing your shoulder blades together and gently lower your head back. Breathe deeply while you hold this stretch for 10 to 15 seconds. Relax the pose and repeat five times.

Energizing stretch

Bring both arms up over your head. Clasp your left hand with your right hand and gently stretch the left side of your body. Breathe deeply while you hold for a count of five. Switch to right side and repeat. Do five sets of stretches.

Happy cow pose

Scoot up to the edge of your seat and place your feet flat on the floor, keeping your knees together. Raise your right arm over your head and bring your left arm down to your side. Bend both arms at the elbows and, bringing your left arm up behind your back, try to join your hands, clasping your fingers. If you can't manage it, just keep your elbows bent and hold this pose for a count of 10 while breathing deeply. Reverse arms and repeat. Do a total of five sets of stretches.

Alternate nostril breathing

Try to do nine sets of this exercise, which is designed to calm and balance the flow of energy through the body. Close your eyes and mouth. Use the thumb of your right hand to close your right nostril. Inhale deeply through your left nostril to a count of 6. Do not exhale yet. Release your right nostril, cover your left nostril, and exhale to a count of 12. Inhale through your right nostril to a count of 6. Exhale through your left nostril to a count of 12.

Deep breathing

Take a deep breath in through your nose, and all the way down into your belly, letting your stomach expand as if it were a balloon. Hold your breath for a few seconds, and then slowly exhale, letting the air out of your stomach, then your lungs, and finally through your nose again. Do several sets.

Restorative pose

Flip down your tray table. Fold your arms on top of it and let your upper body rest on your arms. Try to go as limp as you can. Remember to breathe deeply.

EATING EN ROUTE

If you're on a long flight, you may have ordered a special meal or brought your own food. But what if you're on a short flight where you get only a snack? You could get anything from a bag of peanuts to a sandwich and a tiny red delicious apple.

Beverage Service

Nearly all flights will have beverages. What's the best choice? Whether plain or sparkling, water is always your best choice. Drink at least eight ounces of water for every hour you're in the air to fight dehydration and keep you alert and refreshed.

The caffeine in coffee, tea, or soft drinks will leave you dehydrated and may interrupt your sleep both in the air and after you arrive. Decaffeinated sodas, whether they have sugar or artificial sweetener, can also leave you feeling thirstier than before.

UNHAPPY HOUR

A word of caution about alcohol: It does far more than dehydrate you. The change in air pressure on a plane increases the absorption of alcohol. Drinking one glass of wine or beer on the plane has the same effect as drinking two on the ground. You may be setting yourself up for one nasty hangover when you land.

What about juice? Better, but bear in mind that you may be getting more sugar and sodium than you suspect. Generally, orange and grapefruit juices are fine. Just check to make sure they're 100 percent juice and not artificially sweetened. Tomato juice and V-8 are good choices, particularly if you're hungry. They fill you up and have relatively few calories. But if you're watching your sodium intake, be careful. An average serving can have over 1,000 mg of sodium—almost half the recommended amount of sodium for the whole day.

CARB CURE

Commercial jet cabins are pressurized to 8,000 feet above sea level, creating low air pressure and a high-altitude environment that causes every part of the body to swell, including the digestive track. It's not surprising that you might feel queasy or bloated by the time you land.

To combat this uncomfortable fact of flying, borrow from what mountain climbers have learned about adapting their diets: Avoid fats and proteins and focus on carbohydrates. Carbs are easier to digest and allow the body to function more efficiently at higher altitudes. Pastas, grains, and vegetable salads are a good choice, as are other portable snacks such as rolls or crackers.

Food in the Air

You probably ate before you got on the plane because you know it's best not to travel on an empty stomach. You're still going to be faced with some sort of food choice on the flight. Unless you brought your own snacks, even bags of peanuts can start sounding good after a couple of hours. Part of the problem is often boredom. Sitting in one place for hours (even if you're diligently stretching and exercising throughout the flight) can be downright dull.

Make sure that if you're going to eat something you're truly hungry. Think of your hunger on a scale of 1 to 10–1 being not hungry at all and 10 being ravenous. If you're popping peanuts in your mouth and you're only at a 2 on the scale, it's a waste of calories. If, on the other hand, you figure you're at about a 5, a small snack should suffice. Don't let yourself get to 10 or you're likely to eat your peanuts and your seatmate's, and then ask the flight attendant for more.

Should you snack or have full meals on a flight? It depends on how long the flight is and how you like to eat. If you're a grazer, you may want to snack throughout the flight. If you usually eat three times a day, you'll probably want meals at your usual time. Try to stick to your regular eating schedule. Bringing your own food ensures that you've got something healthy to eat when you're hungry.

FOOD FLIGHT TIPS

If you're going to eat airline food, keep these tips in mind:

☐ Drink eight ounces of water *before* any food is served. Drinking water will make you feel fuller.

☐ Eat the roll without the butter.

☐ For sandwiches, don't bother with the fatty mayonnaise. Use mustard instead.

☐ Take the cheese out of your sandwich and enjoy it with just the meat.

☐ Don't eat the chips and cookies. Eat the fruit. If you're still hungry, ask for another piece.

FIGHTING JET LAG IN THE AIR

While drinking plenty of water, stretching, and exercising are important to counter the effects of jet lag during he flight, sleeping and eating are the main concerns your should address on board. And don't forget to set your watch to your destination time to help get your mind ready.

To Sleep or Not To Sleep?

Whether you should try to sleep on the plane depends on how long you'll be in the air and your arrival time at your destination. If it will be evening when you arrive, you probably shouldn't put in a lot of shut-eye on the plane. You'll be more prepared to fall asleep when it's nighttime at your destination if you haven't slept on the plane. On the other hand, if you're arriving in the morning after a long flight, you should be well rested to face a full day before you can sleep a full night at your destination.

SNOOZE TOOLS

Getting quality sleep on a plane can be difficult with all the distractions. Here are some items that may help:

☐ Sleep mask

☐ Earplugs

☐ Inflatable neck pillow

☐ Blanket, sweater, and socks

Whatever routine you follow before you go to bed at home should be observed while in flight. If brushing your teeth, drinking a glass of water, listening to relaxing music, and reading a book are all precursors to bedding down at home, do them on the plane. Your body is used to the routine and should respond accordingly in the air. Remember that exercising immediately before you try to go to sleep can make it more difficult to fall asleep.

Consider Melatonin

Changing sleeping patterns is a major element in jet lag research. Studies have indicated that melatonin (a hormone produced in the body that helps regulate sleep cycles) can help you sleep on the plane, which may be an effective way to help adjust your sleep cycle to the new time zone. It also helps you adjust more quickly to the new time zone. For advice from other travelers about melatonin, check out the online forum on www.fodors.com.

Try Sleep Aids

If you're one of those people who just can't get any shut-eye on planes, a mild sleeping aid should do the trick. If you opt for a sleeping pill, ask your doctor to prescribe milder drugs such as Ambien or Sonata, as they won't leave you groggy when you arrive. Determine exactly when to take the pill in relation to the length, time, and direction of your flight.

Reset Your Watch

Many experts who study the effects of jet lag agree that setting your watch for your destination's time zone will help you mentally adjust to the time change. You can even begin to live by the new time zone before you leave home. Start changing your sleeping and eating patterns to your destination time. This can be difficult to achieve if you live in a full house, but it's worth a try.

Curtail Alcohol and Caffeine

Steer clear of alcohol and caffeine before and during your flight. Both leave you dehydrated, which exacerbates the symptoms of jet lag. Both also disrupt your sleep, leaving you tired the next day.

Watch What You Eat

What you eat and when you eat it makes it easier to either sleep or stay awake. Proteins will keep you alert, while carbohydrates make you sleepy. If your mission is to stay awake, choose low-fat cheeses or lean meats. If you need to sleep, eat grains like whole wheat bagels or crackers. Stay away from high-fat foods that can require more work from your digestive system and can hinder your efforts to get some shut-eye. Remember the foods that contain tryptophan—turkey, milk, and bananas—help you sleep.

FIGHTING MOTION SICKNESS

Motion sickness is caused by the confusion in the brain between visual cues (what you're seeing) and the information detected in the inner ear (what your body is feeling). Say you're sitting in the back of the plane in an aisle seat. You're not seeing any movement, but your inner ear senses it and sends messages to your brain. Your central nervous system reacts to this confusion by signaling the nausea center in the brain.

If you're susceptible to motion sickness, you can prevent it a few different ways. Medication, such as the over-the-counter drugs Dramamine and Bonine, help suppress the queasiness and nausea. They may also leave you drowsy, however. The drug scopolamine, available in pill form (Scopace) or as a patch (Transderm Scop), also suppresses nausea, but it requires a doctor's prescription. All medications need to be taken an hour before traveling to be effective. If you're struck by motion sickness in the air, it's too late for a pill to do any good.

Other Strategies

If you suffer from motion sickness, you can also:

▶ Choose a seat over the wing of the plane where there's less motion.

▶ Sit by the window so that you will see the same thing that your body feels.

▶ Drink ginger tea 20 minutes before departure, and munch on candied or crystallized ginger during the flight. Studies show ginger reduces symptoms of motion sickness.

▶ Try acupressure. Place the index and middle fingers together an inch down from the base of your palm, on the inside of your wrist. Press down for two to three minutes. Health-food stores also carry wristbands made specifically for this purpose.

▶ Avoid alcohol and greasy foods that can exacerbate symptoms.

AVOIDING GERMS

With so many people crowded into such a confined space, there are bound to be some germs floating around the cabin. Because the air in planes is recirculated, the germs from one cough can spread throughout the entire plane. To protect yourself from these unwelcome traveling companions, take some basic precautions.

▶ Your first lines of defense—the mucous membranes in the eyes, nose, and mouth—suffer from the drying effects of the cabin, which makes it easier for germs to get into your system. Dry mucous membranes can't capture the germs and prevent them from entering your system. Wash your hands and keep them away from your face to significantly lower the risk of infection.

I fly hundreds of thousands of miles each year on business, and I used to catch colds all the time. A few years ago, I started wearing my nifty noise reduction headset on every flight. The headset turns the roar of the engine into soothing white noise. I'm much

TRAVEL LOG

less fatigued, and my resistance to germs has improved tremendously. You can buy them through catalogues or on the Internet.

—Josh G., Boston, Massachusetts

- Drape your own clean pillowcase or towel over the headrest and the airline pillow. Many heads have rested there—let's just leave it at that.
- Personal air purifiers (little gadgets that hang from a string around your neck) are meant to deal with the germs right where they're trying to make their way into the body. The jury's still out on this device, but many people swear by them.

Flying Dry

Dry air plays a critical role in the in-flight germ war zone. When mucous membranes in your eye, nose, and throat are dry, they can't keep germs at bay. Try the antidrying techniques that follow:

- Use a saline nasal spray to lubricate the mucous membranes.
- Cover your nose with a damp cotton handkerchief. This may look a little silly, but it is a terrific strategy for fighting extreme nasal dryness or postflight respiratory illness.
- Drink at least eight ounces of water for every hour in the air. Avoid alcohol and caffeine, which dehydrate you.
- Spritz your face with water to keep your skin moist. Try a prepackaged spritzer, such as the one made by Evian.

I recently began experiencing painful sinus attacks when flying, usually shortly before landing. After some research, I discovered that extremely dry air inside the plane was taxing my swelling sinuses beyond their ability to adapt to

TRAVEL LOG

the decrease in cabin pressure. Other travelers have told me this affects them with sharp pains in the ears, and often happens when they are getting (or already have) a cold. The good news is you can prepare your sinuses by keeping them moist (I prefer natural sea spray), and by taking a decongestant at least a day before flying to keep swelling at bay. Then I take a couple of aspirin the day I fly. I've pretty much licked the problem.

Karen V., Ojai, California

OTHER MODES OF TRANSPORTATION

While most of this chapter has dealt with air travel, you may be wondering about what to do while traveling by car, bus, or train. The good news is that almost all of this information applies to these modes of transportation as well. Whether you're driving or taking a long train trip, just follow the same advice for exercising, eating, drinking, and sleeping en route.

Behind the Wheel

Traveling to your destination by car offers you the luxury of space. Bring fitness gear you might not consider otherwise—bikes, golf clubs, tennis rackets, or skis. Bring more than one type of equipment if you have the room and the time to vary your workout. Don't forget to include all the extras you might need—helmets, shoes, and special clothing for your sport.

Pack a cooler and throw it in the back of the car for your trip. You have the advantage of bringing along perishable foods like low-fat yogurt, so do it. Pull over and take a break to eat your meal. Relax for a bit and then continue your drive without the distraction of fumbling with food containers and wrappers. If you have to stop at a restaurant for food, avoid heavy, fat-laden meals that are hard to digest, as they can make you feel tired while driving.

Stay safe and healthy while you drive with these tips:

► Get out and stretch every two hours or 100 miles. It will help you stay alert.
► Don't drive while taking *any* medication that will make you drowsy. Check warnings on both prescription and over-the-counter medications.
► Avoid long drives during your normal sleeping hours. Your alertness naturally diminishes during this time.
► Exercise along the way with some isometric exercises behind the wheel, or a short jog or walk during a break.
► Take a hint from the U.S. Department of Transportation. The law prohibits truck drivers from being on the road for more than 10 hours a day. Don't extend your driving time longer than this.

By Bus

Packing for bus travel requires some forethought. You can't just grab a sweater out of the trunk, so be prepared to have your carry-on luggage packed with what you'll need—reading material, a personal stereo system, extra layers of clothing, and a small toiletry kit. Keep your personal documents and valuables with you on the bus instead of stowing them away in the luggage compartment.

Follow the same advice on exercise and stretching during airplane travel when you're on a bus. Get up and walk the aisle when you can, and do stretches and isometric exercises to keep your muscles from getting stiff from sitting.

Take food with you, if possible. Since there's no food service on a bus, you're on your own. Pack lots of water and a small cooler filled with healthy snacks. While there may be stops along the way, you don't want to be

CARSICKNESS RX

Besides the familiar medications, the old tried-and-true tricks for beating motion sickness in a car include:

☐ Sit in front, where you will feel less motion. Keep your body and head as still as possible.

☐ Fix your eyes on a distant object.

☐ Get plenty of fresh air as soon as you feel ill.

☐ Don't smoke or drink alcohol before getting in a car, as both can exacerbate the symptoms of motion sickness.

☐ Keep some crackers or saltines handy to munch on. An empty stomach makes motion sickness worse.

famished when you stop at that roadside diner or fast-food franchise.

Riding the Rails

Whether you're going from New York to Boston on Amtrak or from Paris to Istanbul on the Orient Express, observe the same guidelines as for other types of travel. The services offered differ from train to train. While some provide dining cars and sleeping compartments, others may offer just snack bars and reclining seats. Be prepared for whatever you'll face.

Pack your carry-ons the same way you would for air travel. Keep things you need, such as toiletries, reading material, and medications close at hand. For longer trips where you'll want to dress for a meal in the dining car or put on pajamas in your sleeper compartment, pack what you'll need in a small bag that's easier to handle.

One advantage to traveling on a train is that you'll have more space to exercise. Stand up and walk the aisle. Do exercises and stretches. You'll arrive more rested and ready at your destination.

5

Fitness in Your Hotel

YOUR HOTEL IS YOUR HOME BASE for the things you do that are related to your health—everything from getting enough sleep to making sure you take time to exercise. Here's how to maximize your healthy hotel experience.

GOOD NIGHTS

When it comes to staying healthy, sleep is essential. Your body needs time to recharge, especially given the added stress of traveling. Getting enough sleep will also help you combat jet lag, which can affect even the most seasoned traveler for the first few days of a trip.

Stick to your nighttime ritual on the road. Start by setting yourself up for sleep the minute you check in:

- Put your bags in the closet; hang up wrinkle-prone clothing; and stow toiletries in the bathroom.
- Set your room temperature to a cool setting, which improves the environment for sleep.
- Set a favorite photo from home by the bedside.
- Find a radio station to wake up to.
- Call the front desk and arrange for the next morning's wake-up call.
- Plug your night-light in at a strategic spot to guide you to the bathroom in the middle of the night.
- Prep your pillows, lay out your PJs, and ready your book.

All this preparation is so that no matter how full your day or how late your night, you're ready to slip into the routine that will help you sleep.

The Big Sleep

While following your normal bedtime routine is certainly helpful in falling asleep, there are other things you can do as well.

▶ Don't forget your fitness regimen. This will raise your endorphins, help you relax, and give you an all-around good feeling. Don't work out too close to bedtime, though; if you work out an hour or less before hitting the hay you might keep yourself awake.

▶ Request a room away from elevators, stairs, and other noisy areas of the hotel.

▶ Try not to sleep on a full stomach. Avoid stimulants such as alcohol, caffeine, sugar, or nicotine for at least two hours before bedtime.

▶ Give yourself time to decompress from the day's activities.

▶ Don't toss and turn. If you can't sleep, get up. Sit in a chair and read, watch some television, make notes for a meeting, or write letters.

Daytime ZZZs

While getting a good night's sleep is important, 15 or 20-minute power naps during the day can leave you feeling energized. If you're not a napper, you can still rest and get almost the same results. Start by

GETTING COMFORTABLE

Consider these tips for making yourself feel more at home:

☐ Set the temperature controls before you go out to dinner. When you come you'll be ready to jump into bed.

☐ Check the blankets. Are there extras in the closet? If you need more call housekeeping when you arrive.

☐ Are the pillows as soft or as firm as you like them? Do you have enough of them? If not, you should ask for another.

lying still—really still. Recline on your bed or sink into your chair, and let your mind go on a minivacation. Don't let the worries of the day interfere—breathe deeply and picture yourself in a relaxing environment.

KNEAD IT AWAY

More and more hotels offer massages as an added amenity for guests. Be careful, though, as the quality varies. You may get a better massage at the spa or health club down the street. Ask the hotel concierge for the inside scoop on who gives the best massage in the area, and make an appointment as soon as possible.

HOTEL ROOM RX

The air quality in hotel rooms is an increasing concern for many frequent travelers. Mold, mildew, and bacteria inhabiting even the cleanest of rooms can cause a variety of health problems, from allergies to asthma. There are several things you can do to make sure your hotel room environment is as healthful as possible.

The Sniff Test

Stale, allergen-filled air, combined with fumes from common cleaning and deodorizing products can wreak havoc on the well-being of even the healthiest person, causing everything from headaches to sinus attacks to fatigue. Be on the alert for these conditions, and if you smell anything that bothers you, request another room.

Clean scent

Make sure your room smells clean, not overly scented. If you detect the scent of air fresheners, the likely culprit is an ozone-generating device that hides unpleasant odors but leaves mold, mildew, and other contaminants in the air.

Smoke alarm

If you're sensitive to tobacco smoke, be sure there's no hint of it in your room. You may have booked a non-smoking room, but the guest before you may have ignored the rules.

Mold patrol

A damp, musty odor is a sure sign of trouble. Mold and mildew love to live behind vinyl wallpaper (often used in hotels for its looks and durability). You may not see the mold and mildew, but you'll definitely smell it. Hotels located near water are especially susceptible due to the increased humidity, especially on lower floors.

Linens Lessons

After you're in your room, remove the bedspread and put it away in the closet. The bedspreads in hotels aren't laundered as often as the blankets, which in turn are never laundered as often as the sheets. Keep the cleanest bedclothes next to you when you sleep. If you want an extra blanket, ask for one. It's more likely to be freshly laundered. Ask for an extra top sheet to cover the blanket. It's just one more layer of protection against germs and other unpleasantness left behind by guests before you.

BATH RX

Many frequent travelers take a dip—in a bath, a pool, the ocean, a hot tub, or whatever is available—as soon as possible after arriving. Immersing your whole body will help rehydrate you right through your pores.

IN-ROOM EXERCISE

Exercising in your room is one way to stay fit while on the road. If you've brought exercise equipment, use it. The portable dumbbells or exercise video you packed can come out now. Check out the local TV stations for aerobic exercise shows. Presumably these are routines you've developed at home so it should be easy to make it happen in your hotel room.

The following portable hotel room workout doesn't require any special equipment. Write these exercises down on an index card and stick it in your toiletry kit so you'll always have it handy.

Push-ups

Good old-fashioned push-ups—straight or bent-leg—are still the most effective way to strengthen and tone your arms, shoulders, chest—even your abdominals (because you have to keep them tight to do push-ups correctly).

Lie face down on the floor, keeping your hands next to your shoulders. Breathe in, then exhale while pushing your body up. Make sure to keep your abs tight and align your head, neck, and spine throughout the exercise. Lower your body slowly (don't drop your head) until your chest almost touches the floor. Don't rush, or you won't get as much out of the exercise. Return to starting position and repeat 10 times.

Lunges

These are great for the thighs and buttocks. Stand tall with your back straight, hands on hips, and legs shoulder-width apart. Step forward a full stride with your right leg, leading with your heel. Bend your knee until the right leg is at a 90 degree angle to the floor and the left leg is stretched out behind you. Push off with your right leg and return to standing position. Repeat with left leg. Do 10 to 15 lunges per leg, making sure the feet and hips are facing squarely forward throughout the exercise.

Abdominal crunch

Lie flat with your knees bent, your lower back pressed into the floor, and your feet about hip-width apart. Cross your arms over your chest or place your hands lightly on the back of your head (don't interlock your fingers) with your elbows wide. Take a deep breath, and as you exhale, tighten your abs, and curl your head and shoulders off the floor. Hold for a count of two, inhale and slowly lower yourself back down. Repeat for as many sets of 20 crunches as you can manage. Keep your head and neck relaxed throughout the entire set.

Wall squats

For wall squats, which work legs and buttocks, stand with your back and palms against a wall. Slowly slide down, walking your feet away from the wall until they're under you knees—it should look like you're sitting in an invisible chair. Hold for a count of 10 (or until you can't take it anymore) and slowly raise yourself up to a standing position. Take care not to lock your knees at the upright position. Do at least five repetitions.

WORKOUT ON THE GO

If you're limited by what your hotel or the surrounding area has to offer for fitness, be resourceful. Wherever you are, you've got "equipment" at your fingertips.

The phone book

Use the yellow pages to help you work both your arms and calves. First, try some phone book raises for the deltoids and biceps. Stand up straight, knees slightly bent. Hold your arms out in front of you at shoulder height, palms up, with the phone book in the palms of your hands. Raise your arms 2 to 3 inches above shoulder level. Return to shoulder level. Repeat 10 to 15 times. For your calves, use the phone book as a platform for calf-raises. Place the book on the floor and stand on it with your heels hanging over the edge.

Raise your body up until you're on your tiptoes, then lower so that your heels almost touch the floor. Repeat 15 to 20 times.

Your carry-on or briefcase

Use your carry-on or briefcase for some one-arm and standing rows that will work your back. For one-arm rows, rest your left knee and left hand on the edge of your bed, with your right foot planted on the floor. Put your case in your right hand, letting your arm hang with the case near the floor. Slowly bring it up to your ribs, elbow up toward the ceiling. Lower and repeat 15 times. Repeat, resting your right knee and right hand on the edge of the bed, your left foot planted on the floor.

For standing rows, stand up straight, feet a little bit wider than hip-width apart. Hold your case with both hands in front of you, thumbs together. Bend your knees slightly to pull in your pelvis and protect your lower back. Slowly raise the case up to your chest, your elbows out to the sides. Lower and repeat 10 to 15 times.

FUN FITNESS ALTERNATIVES

▶ Biking—Tour the area at a leisurely pace. You'll still get a good workout.
▶ Skating—In-line skating and roller skating are great ways to stay fit. If it's winter, try ice skates.

- Paddle boats—These are an old-fashioned and fun way to see the scenery from the water.
- Row boats—Take turns rowing for a great workout.
- Hiking—Get some information about local hiking areas, pack a daypack, and head for the hills.
- Golf—Pass on the cart and walk the entire course. Many major hotels have their own courses or offer discounts to local courses.
- Tennis—Get a group together for doubles.
- Dancing—Find a local club and dance the night away. Learn a new type of move, such as salsa or merengue. Take a hula lesson—when in Hawaii, definitely do as the Hawaiians do.

Stretching

A leisurely 15-minute stretching routine can leave you feeling invigorated and ready to get on with your day. Add the stretches described here to those mentioned in Chapters 3 and 4.

Cat stretch

This works the chest, shoulders, and back. On all fours on the floor, with your knees about shoulder-width apart, walk your hands out in front of you about a foot. Shift your weight back toward your hips (as if you're trying to sit on your legs), press your chest toward the floor, with arms straight out in front of you, almost flat on the floor. Hold for 30 seconds.

Knee hug

This relaxing stretch is for legs, hips, and lower back. Lie on your back with legs extended. Pull right leg up toward your chest, grabbing it behind the knee with both arms. While keeping your hips and upper back flat on the floor, gently pull your right leg toward your chest. Hold for 30 seconds, lower, and repeat with left leg.

Seal stretch

This exercise stretches your chest, abs, and lower back. Lie on your stomach. Slowly push your chest up, straightening your arms, keeping your hips and legs on the ground and your neck in line with your shoulders. Hold for a count of 10, and lower yourself back to the floor.

Long stretch

To strengthen your back and arms, lie flat on the floor on your stomach with your forehead on the floor and your arms and legs extended Superman-style. Slowly raise your right arm and left leg about an inch off the floor, keeping your hips on the floor. Make your body as long as possible. Hold for a count of 5. Lower, and repeat with left arm and right leg.

The Pool

If your hotel has a pool, you may find it difficult to swim laps unless you get there before the families with children claim it as their own. Even if you do get up early, you may find the pool is too short to get a good workout. But there are other ways to exercise in the pool using the natural resistance of the water to tone muscles.

Arm press

To work out your upper back, stand with your knees slightly bent, shoulders below water level. Bring your hands in front of you, shoulder height and palms together. Keeping your elbows straight, sweep your arms behind you as far as you can, squeezing your shoulder blades together. Sweep back to starting position. Do this 20 times.

Criss-cross

For the chest and shoulders, stand with knees slightly bent, shoulders below water level. Stretch your arms in front of you, crossing at the elbow. Pull your arms back, stopping at your side. Move your arms back to starting position, crossing the opposite way. Repeat 20 times.

Bicep curl/triceps press

Stand with your knees slightly bent, shoulders below water level, arms by your sides, fists facing forward.

Slowly curl your arms up, as if you're raising a dumb-bell. When you reach the top of the curl, turn your fists in the other direction and push arms downward to work triceps. Return to starting position and repeat 20 times.

Ab tuck

In shoulder-deep water, lean your back against the pool wall, extend your arms out to your sides, and hold the edge of the pool. Contract your abs and lift your knees to your chest. Return to starting position. Repeat 20 times.

I'm a swimmer and one of my best memories is of staying at the Claremont Hotel in Berkeley, California. The outdoor pool, which is heated, opens at 5 AM. In the winter, it's still dark when the pool opens, so I swam under a full moon in the dark with the scent of redwoods and euca-lyptus. It was such a magical way to stay in shape, I did 10 extra laps without even realizing.

TRAVEL LOG

—Nancy B., Duluth, Minnesota

Lunges

Stand with your feet hip-width apart, knees slightly bent, arms by your sides, in shoulder-deep water. Step forward with your left foot into a lunge position, raising your arms in front of you to shoulder height. Return to starting position and repeat 20 times on each leg.

Kicks

Float on your stomach in shoulder-deep water, holding on to the edge of the pool. Tighten your abs and gluts, then start scissor-kicking your legs below the surface of the water. Do this for one minute, rest for 15 seconds, then repeat. Do a total of six minutes of kicking.

Aerobic exercise

The pool is a great place for aerobic exercise as well. Try jogging in place and doing jumping jacks in the shallow end, or treading water in the deep end. You'll be moving slower than on land, but you've got the added benefit of the water resistance for a complete workout.

All in the Timing

If you don't have time for a long workout, it might be easier to do five or six 5-minute workouts. It's not hard to rack up 25 or 30 minutes of exercise a day by sneaking it in when you can.

The best overall way to spend five minutes is walking. The key here is to walk like you mean it—don't just stroll. And don't forget isometric exercises, which can be done in an elevator, while waiting for a cab, or while standing in line at a deli. Take a few minutes and do some head rolls, shoulder shrugs, and ankle rotations.

Rise and Shine

An easy way to make sure you get exercise into your day is to get up a bit earlier. Wake up an hour earlier to get in a 45-minute run before breakfast. If the hotel gym or pool opens early, head down for some laps.

I've gotten into the habit of doing power walks very early in the morning instead of waiting around for the hotel gym to open. It's a great way to squeeze in a little sight-seeing during a busy business trip. I've covered Milan, Geneva, and Paris in

TRAVEL LOG

a few hours and I get to see early morning activities that regular tourists miss. I also avoid the pollution from heavy traffic later in the day.

—*Gordon C., Dallas, Texas*

It took me years to get into shape, so when we were planning to vacation in the south of France, I was worried that I would return to my slothful ways. On our first day in Aixen-Provence, I spotted a shop sign that read "Gym Concept." The club was for locals, but I was able to take four or five aerobics classes on a drop-in basis. The classes were in French, but I could follow the instructor fairly well. And I added the words for abdomen and thigh to my limited French vocabulary. My favorite classmate was a chic woman who rushed in late for class, reeking of cigarette smoke, and changed into her gym clothes in the middle of the room. And I'm sure she rushed off to the local wine bar right afterward. Vive la France!

TRAVEL LOG

—*Helen G., Menlo Park, California*

Even getting up 15 minutes earlier allows time for stretching (here's where the yoga tape you packed will come in handy).

Lunch Laps

Lunch is a perfect time to fit in a little exercise. Of course you shouldn't skip a meal, but you can trade the coffee and dessert for a brisk walk. Explore the neighborhood around your hotel. Rent a bike and ride through a nearby park. Find a quiet spot and stretch. Or head to the gym and grab a quick workout during your lunch hour. You can be in and out in less than an hour.

The Bottom Line

At the very least, plan a 15-minute stretch before you set off for a day of meetings or touring. Later in the day, make time for 30 minutes of exercise—outdoors, in the gym, or in your room—followed by a relaxing swim in the hotel pool, a soak in the hot tub, or a hot bath. You'll feel great, sleep well, and have all the energy you need.

6

Dining on the Road

NOTHING GETS A HEALTH AND fitness program off track more quickly than the foods typically found at vacation resorts or convention hotels. Even the most seasoned traveler can fall victim to "Hey, why not?" thinking. Dining out may subject you to temptations you would have avoided at home, in the form of heavy, rich meals that can quickly add up to unwanted pounds.

ABCs OF EATING

There *are* better ways to treat yourself than indulging. To avoid the pitfalls of dining on the road, keep these ABCs mind.

A is for adapt

Don't just abandon your healthy eating habits when you hit the road—tweak them a bit. Focus on staying within your normal daily range for calories, fat, carbs, and protein. Follow your regular eating patterns as closely as you can. When your regular habits have to bend with the inevitable variables of travel, look for the next opportunity to get back on track.

B is for balance

The trick is to see the big picture when it comes to food. Eating right is an ongoing process, from the first bite of breakfast in the morning to the last bite of dinner in the evening. Keep a mental log of the foods you eat while traveling. If you've had a big lunch, balance it with a smaller dinner. If you didn't have time for your usual breakfast, grab an apple as a midmorning snack. Save some calories during the day so you won't feel guilty about that big night out on the town. And while you're keeping an eye on your calorie intake, make sure the food you consume has a balance of nutrients to keep you fit and healthy.

C is for control

Why does a healthy diet go out the window when you travel? Because you're at the mercy of the menu. Or are you? A menu is printed on paper, not written in stone. Whether you ask for a menu item to be grilled instead of fried, steamed instead of sautéed, you do have a choice. Stay in control.

RESTAURANT RULES

Let's face it—menus are made to entice you. Even fast-food restaurants whose menus are plastered on a wall show pictures of tempting treats. While you may intend

MAKE THE MOST OF YOUR MEAL

☐ Don't starve yourself during the day if you're going out to dinner in the evening. You'll be ravenous, which will make you susceptible to overeating. Have a light breakfast and lunch, and a small snack and a big glass of water a few hours before dinner.

☐ If you order a higher calorie entrée, balance it with a lower calorie starter. Make sure to eat the lower calorie item first.

☐ Eat only what you order. Push away all the extras placed on the table before the meal, from bread to crackers to chips. Better yet, ask the wait staff to take them away.

☐ Eat slowly—enjoy the taste of the food.

to eat healthfully when you get to the restaurant, the menu itself can break your resolve.

Ordering without looking at the menu may sound crazy, but it works. The National Restaurant Association states that three out of four restaurants are happy to modify the way their food is prepared if requested. The key is to know what you want before you walk in the door. When you're thinking about what to ask for, imagine you're at home and the fridge is full of healthy foods. Picture the meal you might make for yourself and then describe it to your server. You might, for instance, ask for a piece of grilled Chilean sea bass with

---

We never let diets follow us on vacation. Instead, we tend to walk a lot and stay fit by going to hotel gyms, jogging, and playing tennis. While we avoid buffets (at home, too) we would never refuse to sample

TRAVEL LOG

a local dessert, wine, or entrée that *must* be tasted. That's what vacations are for. Key West? Key lime pie! Paris? Crêpes and croissants!

—*Marguerite L., Grand Rapids, Michigan*

---

an herb sauce, some lemon rice, and lightly steamed broccoli. The waitperson may try to point you to an item on the menu that is similar to what you've requested and that's fine, as long as it suits your specifications. In better restaurants, the chef will be more than willing to work with you.

Choosing a Restaurant

Take some time to consider where you'll eat. Don't just hope the restaurant near your hotel will have healthy fare—do your homework. Theoretically you've scoped out restaurants before leaving home. If you haven't, you have some extra tools at your disposal.

Check in with the concierge at the hotel for recommendations. The hotel may even have menus from

EATING HEALTHY CHINESE STYLE

- ☐ Banish crunchy fried noodles from the table.
- ☐ Ask for the meal to be prepared without MSG, salt, or extra soy sauce.
- ☐ Order clear, broth-type soups like wonton, egg drop, and hot and sour soups.
- ☐ Avoid dishes that are breaded or deep-fried. Be on the lookout for foods called "crispy" and "crunchy."
- ☐ Order steamed rice instead of fried.
- ☐ Ask for simple steamed vegetable dishes.

area restaurants that you can peruse. Don't be afraid to call a restaurant before venturing out to make sure you're not wasting your time.

If you're careful to avoid heavy sauces or fried foods, you can have a heart-healthy treat with foreign cuisine. Vietnamese, Indian, and Chinese menus emphasize vegetables and grains. Meat, if used at all, is as an accent flavor. Just make sure you ask them to go easy on the oil.

Fish is always a good choice, so seek out seafood restaurants. Just be sure to get it steamed, grilled, broiled, or poached. "Broiled dry" is how to order it so it's not swimming in butter.

EATING HEALTHY ITALIAN STYLE

- ☐ Ask for salad dressing on the side or ask for oil and vinegar at the table.

- ☐ Substitute chicken or veal for sausage.

- ☐ Grab a slice. Pizza isn't so bad if you stay away from the pepperoni, sausage, and other fatty meats. Ask them to lighten up on the cheese, or skip it entirely.

- ☐ Ask for salads without cheese, steamed fish, chicken or veal that has been roasted or grilled, bean or vegetable soups, and pasta with vegetables, marinara sauce, or seafood.

Most sandwich shops offer healthful ingredients, as well as the calorie- and fat-loaded ones. Sliced meats such as turkey and chicken are usually lower in fat. Keep away from the processed meats like bologna, salami, and liverwurst. Hold the mayonnaise and oil, but pile on the mustard, lettuce, tomato, sprouts, onions, and peppers.

MENU MAGIC

Certain words in menu descriptions immediately clue you in to how a restaurant prepares its food. Some buzzwords point to foods prepared with extra fat and some signal preparations that should help you in your quest for health.

Heavy Buzzwords

▶ Au gratin
▶ Beurre blanc
▶ Pastry-wrapped
▶ Buttered, butter sauces
▶ Breaded, lightly breaded
▶ Newburg
▶ Bisque
▶ Cheese sauce
▶ Fried
▶ Crispy
▶ Cream
▶ Scalloped
▶ Sautéed
▶ Tempura

Healthy Buzzwords

▶ Au jus
▶ Baked
▶ Broiled
▶ Grilled
▶ Roasted
▶ Steamed
▶ Poached
▶ Garden-fresh
▶ Marinara sauce
▶ Raw (in the developed world)

Safe Dining

If you're traveling in countries where the quality of the water is a concern, you need to take precautions when dining out. The old traveler's adage that says a food is fine "if you can peel it, cook it, or boil it" is on target. This will help keep you out of dangerous situations. Assume that restaurants use the local water in food preparation.

▶ Stay away from raw fruits and vegetables—they may have been washed in unclean water.

▶ Drink only bottled beverages that are still sealed when served.

▶ Don't use ice cubes that may have been made with unclean water—drink your beverage warm if necessary.

▶ Don't drink instant coffee and tea—the water may not have been boiled.

▶ Never eat raw or undercooked fish, meat, or eggs. Make sure these items aren't disguised in sauces or stews.

▶ Be sure the meal you get is hot—food that is room temperature has probably been sitting for a while.

▶ Be careful when buying food from street vendors. Make sure the food is prepared in front of you.

▶ Eat only fruits you can peel yourself, like bananas and oranges.

At the Table

There are other ways to keep your meals healthy. Don't keep eating until you feel full, as it can take up to 20 minutes for your brain to register that you've had enough. Engage in conversation. Eat slowly and savor every bite. Leave something on your plate—your mother might disagree but there is no rule that says you have to eat everything. If you have a fridge in your room, take leftovers back to the hotel and have them for lunch the next day.

EATING HEALTHY MEXICAN STYLE

☐ Ask the staff to remove the tortilla chips from the table.

☐ Hold the sour cream, cheese, and guacamole. Use fresh salsa instead.

☐ Choose soft flour tortillas over fried corn ones.

☐ Good choices are black bean soup or gazpacho, chicken with rice, tostadas, fajitas, and steamed tamales.

Appealing Appetizers

Appetizers may be smaller than entrées, but they can still be loaded with calories. Take Buffalo chicken wings. One order of these tempting, deep-fried, blue-cheese-drenched morsels weighs in at more than 1,000 calories and has anywhere from 100 to 200 percent of your recommended daily allowance of fat.

If there's an appetizer you can't resist, share it with a friend. Select two healthy appetizers instead of an entrée. If you want soup, choose one that's clear or tomato-based—the cream-based ones are surefire diet-busters.

Best Beverage Bets

Always have water on the table. Drinking water throughout the meal helps you feel full, so you'll eat less. Ask for a pitcher so you can refill your own glass as often as you like. If you're having a cocktail, take sips of water in between sips of your drink. If you're having a glass of wine or beer, order it with dinner instead of having one glass before and another during your meal. Or have a wine spritzer—wine mixed with club soda—to start. Keep after-dinner coffee to a minimum—or skip it altogether—so you won't have trouble falling asleep.

THE TRUTH ABOUT JOE

When you're traveling, you're more likely to drop by Starbucks for a caffeine jolt. But the average fat and calorie content of most coffee bar offerings is off the charts—a 16-ounce whole-milk latte can have 200 calories and 5 or more grams of fat. So reconsider the chai lattes, iced mochas, and other rich and frothy coffee beverages. If you can't do without the milk, stick with nonfat and save your calories for a more memorable treat.

Salad Daze

Salads are great—until you add the dressing, croutons, nuts, and seeds. Try ordering your salad without the extras. Always ask for the dressing on the side. Dip your fork into the dressing before each bite instead of smothering the whole salad—you'll be amazed at how much will be left over. Choose low-fat dressing or oil and vinegar, or try lemon and pepper for a zingy fat-free dressing.

CARBO AVOIDING

The basket of freshly baked bread is tempting. But remember that a single dinner roll or slice of bread can have 100 calories or more. It's easy to idly rack up hundreds of calories before your entrée arrives. And one pat of butter (usually a tablespoon) can add a whopping 12 grams of fat and 100 calories to your meal. Tortilla chips aren't any better. Just a handful can have 130 calories and 6 grams fat.

Eat Your Cake?

When it comes to dessert, sherbet, sorbet, and fresh fruits are your best bets. But, if the crème brûlée is calling your name, go ahead and order it. Just be sure to ask for extra forks so you can share with your dinner companions. Better yet, ask one of your companions if

TIPS TO LIGHTEN ANY MENU

- ☐ Order a clear soup or consommé for an appetizer.
- ☐ Ask that the bread and butter be removed from the table.
- ☐ Order meat broiled, grilled, poached, or roasted.
- ☐ Ask for half of your portion to be wrapped up for a take-away bag before your entrée is served.
- ☐ Order extra vegetables.
- ☐ Have a salad and an appetizer for your meal.
- ☐ Refuse high-fat side dishes such as fries, chips, or potato salad.
- ☐ Order seltzer with a slice of lemon or lime instead of a soft drink.
- ☐ Ask for extra forks for sharing dessert.
- ☐ Always leave something on your plate.

you can share theirs. That way you won't feel obliged to clean the plate.

HEALTHY SNACKING

Snacking is a *good* thing. It can help keep your diet on track by keeping your blood sugar levels more constant, decreasing food cravings. But this only works if you make your snack choices carefully. Pick foods that will give you energy—not a candy bar, which will leave you feeling run-down after that initial sugar rush. Fruit, vegetables, whole wheat crackers and bagels, raisins, and sports bars are all good choices. They're easily portable so you can tuck them in your daypack or briefcase. Popcorn (*without* butter), rice cakes, and fat-free pretzels are other snacks that won't short-circuit your diet goals.

BUY YOUR OWN FOOD

If you'll be away more than a few days, use your hotel minibar to help you stick to your eating program. Stop at the supermarket or health-food store and stock up on healthy snacks. Fresh fruit, yogurt, skim milk, mineral water, and low-fat cottage cheese will keep you going

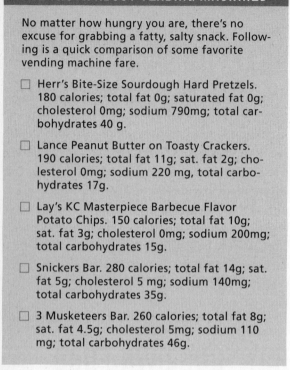

THE TRUTH ABOUT VENDING MACHINES

No matter how hungry you are, there's no excuse for grabbing a fatty, salty snack. Following is a quick comparison of some favorite vending machine fare.

☐ Herr's Bite-Size Sourdough Hard Pretzels. 180 calories; total fat 0g; saturated fat 0g; cholesterol 0mg; sodium 790mg; total carbohydrates 40 g.

☐ Lance Peanut Butter on Toasty Crackers. 190 calories; total fat 11g; sat. fat 2g; cholesterol 0mg; sodium 220 mg, total carbohydrates 17g.

☐ Lay's KC Masterpiece Barbecue Flavor Potato Chips. 150 calories; total fat 10g; sat. fat 3g; cholesterol 0mg; sodium 200mg; total carbohydrates 15g.

☐ Snickers Bar. 280 calories; total fat 14g; sat. fat 5g; cholesterol 5 mg; sodium 140mg; total carbohydrates 35g.

☐ 3 Musketeers Bar. 260 calories; total fat 8g; sat. fat 4.5g; cholesterol 5mg; sodium 110 mg; total carbohydrates 46g.

anytime during the day. Use your supplies to eat one meal a day in your room. Breakfast is a good bet—have cereal with skim milk and fresh fruit, top a whole wheat bagel with low-fat cream cheese, or pair a container of yogurt with some whole-grain crackers. Mornings are usually rush-time, so having breakfast at your fingertips can be a major time-saver.

You can keep low-fat sandwich meats in the refrigerator for a quick lunch or dinner. Many grocery stores offer prepared sandwiches that you can store until you're ready to eat them. Keep a supply of instant

BREAKFAST BINGE-BUSTERS

While you're traveling, if you must eat breakfast in a restaurant, skip the all-you-can-eat buffet. If you can't avoid the buffet, be mentally prepared for it. Go straight for things you'd have ordered off the menu or from room service.

- [ ] Toast (whole wheat, raisin, or rye) without butter
- [ ] Yogurt and fruit
- [ ] Hot or cold cereal with skim milk and a banana
- [ ] French toast made with egg whites
- [ ] Egg-white or egg-substitute omelette with vegetables
- [ ] Plain poached egg whites on a plain English muffin
- [ ] Pancakes without butter, topped with fresh fruit
- [ ] Grapefruit and other citrus fruits

soups and cereals if you have access to hot water from room service or in-room facilities.

BON APPETIT

The point of all this strategizing is to keep you from abandoning your health and fitness program when you're on the road. This isn't to say you shouldn't enjoy yourself. Exercise, eat well, have fun. You'll return home rested, relaxed, and looking forward to your next trip.

Fitness Resources

Fodor's Resources

Guidebooks

Fodor's Healthy Escapes

Helps you choose among hundreds of spas and resorts across the USA, Mexico, and the Caribbean.

Fodor's Skiing USA

Reviews slopes, trails, inns, and restaurants, and après-ski activities at the country's top ski resorts.

Golf Digest's Places to Play

Rates 6,000 public and resort courses, and includes all the details you need to plan a golf vacation.

On the Web

fodors.com

A great place to start planning a healthy vacation. You can search for hotels with spas, swimming pools, and other sports facilities, and for restaurants by cuisines. In the Travel Talk section of the site, you can also post your most specific questions and hear answers from your fellow travelers.

Medical Assistance

International Association for Medical Assistance to Travelers

417 Center Street
Lewiston, NY 14092
716/754-4883
sentex.net/iamat

Centers for Disease Control and Prevention

1600 Clifton Road
Atlanta, GA 30333
General information:
800/311-3435
Travelers information:
877/394-8747
cdc.gov

World Health Organization

525 23rd Street, NW
Washington, DC 20037
202/861-3200
who.int

More Web Sites

Encyclozine

encyclozine.com
Links to sites on cycling and hiking. The site also helps you make reservations.

Fitscape

fitscape.com
Information about exercise (workout programs, animated exercise instructions), nutrition (a food and nutrition calculator), and a feature that lets you search for health clubs in destinations all over the world.

Great Outdoor Recreation Pages

gorp.com
Includes all kinds of tools to help you plan active vacations.

Just Move

justmove.org
Run by the American Heart Association, this free site gives you a digital diary, weekly motivational updates, and support from other exercise aficionados across the country.

Running.com

running.com
Lists places to run, races around the world, and general running information.

Swimmers Guide Online

lornet.com/sgol
Directory of publicly accessible, full-size, year-round pools available in 91 countries.

U.S. State Department Travel

travel.state.gov
The U.S. State Department keeps you up-to-date on visa requirements and safety issues all over the world.

VegDining

vegdining.com
Guide to vegetarian restaurants around the world.

Weight Watchers International

800/651-6000
weightwatchers.com
Includes tips on healthy eating and staying fit. Also features tips from readers on sticking to their diet plans.

Yoga Movement

yogamovement.com
Features yoga basics for beginners, resources for pros, and links to other yoga sites.

Product Catalogs

Athleta

888/322-5515
athleta.com
Fitness and sports gear for women.

Living

800/254-8464
gaiam.com
Yoga videos and other relaxation products for travel.

Power Systems

800/321-6975
power-systems.com
Portable exercise equipment that can easily fit in your suitcase.

Road Runner Sports

800/551-5558
roadrunnersports.com
Clothes, shoes, and accessories for men and women interested in running, jogging, and walking.

Travel Agencies

Adventure Health Travel

800/443-9216

adventurehealthtravel.com

This online division of a 50-year-old agency specializes in spas, fitness, and adventure vacations.

Fitness Travel Club

hotelfitnessclub.com

Members can search online for hotels with health clubs and spas.

Journeys Expeditions and Voyages, Inc.

509/884-4940

Specializes in active, adventurous, or rejuvenating vacations.

Spa Finder

800/255-7727

spafinder.com

On its Web site, the world's largest spa travel and reservation company lets you search for spas and resorts.

Spaquest

800/772-7837

spa-quest.com

Provides all the specifics you need to complete a spa reservation.

Travel and Fitness Magazines

Metro Sports

27 West 24th Street, Suite 10B
New York, NY 10010
212/627-7040

metrosports.com

Monthly magazines in New York, Boston, Philadelphia, and Washington, D.C. guide readers to participatory events, sports travel destinations, and local high-end retailers. Issues include coverage of running, in-line skating, hockey, basketball, hiking, and other sports.

Runners World

800/666-2828

runnersworld.com

Monthly features on runs around the world.

Travel Gear

eBags
800/820-6126
ebags.com
*Sells all types of luggage,
including types easier on your
body.*

Ex Officio
800/644-7303
exofficio.com
*Sells clothing for excursions
with harsher weather
conditions.*

Magellan's
800/962-4943
magellans.com
*Markets travel gear, from jet-
lag prevention medicine to
aquatic dumbbells.*

Sharper Image
800/344-5555
sharperimage.com
*Sells range of travel gear from
luggage to alarm clocks.*

Travelsmith
800/950-1600
travelsmith.com
*Sells lightweight, easy-to-pack
travel clothes.*

Yoga Enterprises
888/YES-YOGA
stretch.com
*"In-Flight Yoga" and "Bed
Top Yoga," and other audio
tapes are available.*

Travel Insurance

Access America
800/284-8300

CSA
800/348-9505

Travel Guard
800/826-1300

Notes

Notes

Notes

Notes

Notes

Notes

Fodor's
Key to the Guides

America's guidebook leader publishes guides for every kind of traveler—check out our many series and find your perfect match.

Fodor's Gold Guides
America's best-selling travel guide series offers the most detailed insider reviews of hotels, restaurants, and attractions in all price ranges, plus great background information, smart tips, useful maps, and more.

Fodor's Road Guide USA
Big guides for a big country—the most comprehensive guides to America's roads, packed with places to stay, eat, and play across the USA. Just right for road warriors, family vacationers, cross-country trekkers, and anyone hitting the road.

COMPASS AMERICAN GUIDES
Stunning guides from top local writers and photographers—gorgeous photos, literary excerpts, colorful anecdotes, and more. A must-have for culture mavens, history buffs, and new residents.

Fodor's CITYPACKS
Concise city coverage with a fold-out map. The right choice for urban travelers who want everything under one cover.

Fodor's EXPLORING GUIDES
Hundreds of color photos bring your destination to life; lively stories share insight into the culture, history, and people. Great for independent explorers who want in-depth background coverage.

ADDITIONAL GUIDES →

Fodor's POCKET GUIDES
For travelers who don't need as much information—the best of Fodor's in pocket-size packages for just $10.

Fodor's To Go
Credit-card sized, magnetic color microguides that fit right in the palm of your hand—perfect for "stealth" travelers or as gifts.

Fodor's FLASHMAPS
Every resident's map guide: 60 easy-to-follow maps: public transit, parks, museums, zip codes, and more.

Fodor's CITYGUIDES
Sourcebooks for living in the city: Thousands of in-the-know listings for restaurants, shops, sports, nightlife, and other city resources.

Fodor's AROUND THE CITY WITH KIDS
Great ideas for family days in your own backyard or on the road.

Fodor's upCLOSE
Travel well, spend less with these lively guides for travelers who crave value and want to get away from the crowds.

Fodor's ESCAPE
Fill your trip with once-in-a-lifetime experiences, from ballooning in Chianti to overnighting in the Moroccan desert. These full-color dream books point the way.

Fodor's Languages for Travelers
Learn the local language before hitting the road. Available in Phrase Books or Audio Sets.

Karen Brown's Guides
Engaging guides to the most charming inns and B&Bs in the USA and Europe, with easy-to-follow inn-to-inn itineraries.

Baedeker's Guides
Comprehensive guides trusted since 1829, packed with A–Z reviews and star ratings.

Need to JUMP-START
your fitness program?

In the mood for a little *pampering*?

Check out **Fodor's** HEALTHY ESCAPES and check into one of the hundreds of spas and fitness resorts covered in this one-of-a-kind guide. You'll get the lowdown on the best facilities in the United States, Canada, Mexico, and the Caribbean, with detailed information on accommodations, rates, and special programs. No matter what kind of escape you're planning—from luxury pampering to sports conditioning to slimming down—**HEALTHY ESCAPES** makes getting there a breeze.

Fodor's HEALTHY ESCAPES
284 Resort and Retreats Where You Can Get Fit, Feel Good, Find Yourself, and Get Away from It All